maria luisa frisa

italian fashion now

Marsilio FONDAZIONE PITTI DISCOVERY

many thanks to:
Angelo Sensini Communication
Alessia Barrera
Alice Bon
Olivier Bourgis
Valentina Bruni
Marco Brusamolin
Véronique Chalmeton
Guilhem Charneau
Pauline Chavel
Emanuela Consoli
Dainese
Chiara Dalla Stella
Martina D'Amato
Enrico Della Svizzera
Cristina de Rosas
Cristina Ferrari
Gianfranco Ferré
Gabriele Giorgini
Luisella Giraudo
Givenchy
Grifoni Denim
Katerina Godi
Gucci
Daniele Guidetti
Guitar
Guy Rover
Halston
Elena Indiano
Italia Independent
Karla Otto
Anna Larese
Anna Locatelli
Mehak Luthra
Francesca Maiorani
Maximilian Linz Press and Public Relations
Letizia Montani Fargna
Tersilia Musso
Nathu
Sarah Nowak
Morgan O'Donovan
Leila Palermo
Angela Paoli
Stefano Pitigliani
Roberta Raccagni
Rochas
Roberto Roncalli
Salvatore Ferragamo
Mila Schön
Michela Serlenga
Mara Sgualdi
Siddharta Shukla
Tiziana Solito
Studio Next
Valentino
Vionnet
Yves Saint Laurent
Z Zegna

texts of the section
profiles: in loose, order
Angelo Flaccavento

design and visual editing
Alessandro Gori.Laboratorium

MMXI

general coordination
Serena Becagli.Laboratorium

translation
Huw Evans

The tracks sequence is
composed by images taken
from youtube and the web.
On pp. 36-37 screenshot from
the video *Manifesto VII* by Inez
van Lamsweerde and Vinoodh
Matadin of the collection Yves
Saint Laurent FW 2010-2011;
on p. 68 screenshot from the
video by Giampaolo Sgura
of the collection Francesco
Scognamiglio FW 2010-2011;
on pp. 82-83 photo by
Frederique Dumoulin of the
collection Givenchy haute
coutere SS 2007

The Fondazione Pitti Discovery
regrets if the credits for any
of the photographs have been
involuntarily omitted and is at
the disposal of any copyright
holder

© 2011 by Fondazione Pitti
Discovery
© 2011 by Marsilio Editori® s.p.a.,
Venice
www.marsilioeditori.it

first edition: February 2011
isbn 88-317-9812

no part of this publication
may be produced stored in a
retrieval system or transmitted
in any form or by means
without the prior permission
writing of the copyright holder
ande the publisher

printed by Grafiche Siz s.p.a.,
Campagnola di Zevio (Verona)
for Marsilio Editori® s.p.a., Venice

In line with the aims of making the world of fashion accessible to the general public that the Fondazione Pitti Discovery, in collaboration with Marsilio, has set itself with the Mode series, this new book by Maria Luisa Frisa proposes a survey of new Italian fashion, i.e. of the latest generations of Italian fashion designers working in this country or abroad and who are, as they say, making a significant mark on international fashion. The result is a mosaic or a map—let readers choose the metaphor they prefer—of a rich and varied movement that highlights some very personal talents and styles but also brings out some common characteristics and sensibilities. It is important to talk about this movement even though it is not possible to give it a precise label. Firstly, because perhaps more than ever before Italy is in need at this moment in history of a collective self-awareness in one of the most important areas of the modern, truly successful culture of creative design; secondly, because a better understanding of ourselves is the indispensable condition for the gaze of others to focus with greater attention and I would say even with renewed surprise on our work and our qualities.

Lapo Cianchi
Segretary-General Fondazione Pitti Discovery

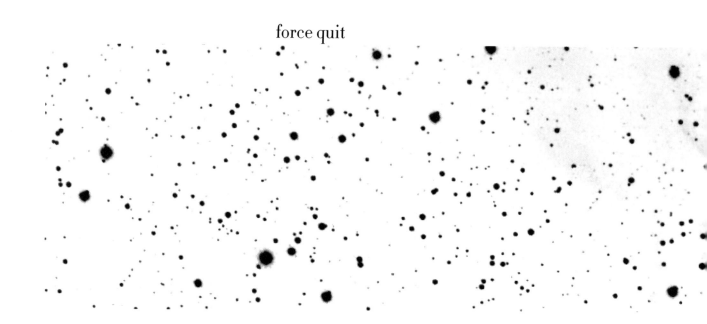
force quit

I

IF NO ONE ASKS ME, I KNOW WHAT IT IS. IF I WISH TO EXPLAIN IT TO HIM WHO ASKS, I DO NOT KNOW.

(St. Augustine, CONFESSIONS)

There are many reasons why I decided to embark on the dangerous adventure of putting together a book on the Italian fashion of the younger generations. Not on the history of fashion, but on fashion as a work in progress. First of all there is undoubtedly the need to take stock of a situation where important things are going on, but which for a series of reasons is not succeeding in making the impact that it should. It is unable to gel around the expression of a sort of movement that exists at an unconscious level, but only becomes visible and comprehensible as a whole when you take a step back and look at the individual experiences from a distance. A constellation that is revealed at the moment in which the routes that have been followed are traced and that can then be grasped and shared not just by critics, the press and experts, and as a consequence the public too, but also by the designers themselves, who are conscious of the importance of system building. So what is needed is a sort of manifesto that would lay out, despite all the differences, a project, a vision, as well as an identity, a common root: characteristics that, when pointed out, lead to talk of a group, despite the generational differences, just as is already happening in our country for artists, movie directors or writers.[1]

Where fashion is concerned, however, it seems that in Italy–after the great protagonists of the period which goes under the label of "Made in Italy" (Giorgio Armani, Gianni Versace, Gianfranco Ferré and Krizia, to mention just a few names) and after the designers like Romeo Gigli or Dolce & Gabbana who emerged just after that exhilarating time–something has got stuck. The capacity has been lost to stay on the front line, operating in the present time and in keeping with what is going on in the rest of the world, but defined within that Italian character which is rooted in quality fabrics, perfect cuts, balanced volumes and a manufacturing process where care is taken over the smallest details that are then put to the test of industrial production.

Thus it appears that these characteristics, ingrained in the important Italian tradition of craftsmanship (unique of its kind), in its constant capacity to transform itself and adapt itself to the needs of production, instead of being an asset, a solid base from which to set off in new directions, are a kind of straitjacket that blocks all movement. A straitjacket imposed, without encountering much resistance, on Italy by a sort of general opinion that sees it above all as the place of superlative production. Another reason is my conviction of the need to reflect on Italian contemporary fashion in a critical manner, trying to look at it from the perspective and with the means that derive from my having been an art critic in times when the talk was of militancy, when the last generation was

---

[1] Writers in Italy, for example, have recently succeeded in forming themselves into a body, at once united and diverse, capable of producing in the subjects that they deal with narrations which are "grand, ambitious, far-reaching, wide-ranging and all the expressions that come to mind." This is what Asor Rosa wrote in 2009, backing up his claim by citing the words of the Wu Ming collective in its *New Italian Epic* (Alberto Asor Rosa, "Ritorno in Provincia. Le cento Italie dei giovani scrittori," in *la Repubblica*, December 15, 2009; Wu Ming, *New Italian Epic. Letteratura, sguardo obliquo, ritorno al futuro*; Turin: Einaudi, 2009).

always antagonistic toward the previous one and put itself to the test in the territories of the underground. Conscious, above all, of the importance of firsthand experience, of the need to be there, of the logic of taking risks and having fun. With an awareness of the necessity of sharing and of the fact that it is not possible to make it on your own. A way of imagining, so as to plan ahead, but especially to be with others, finding a thousand good reasons to continually bring yourself into question, in a research that will take you outside preestablished schemes, in order to understand what is happening and be sensitive to what is in the air. Criticism is chiefly a work of photography, an attempt to get an overall picture while being ready to zoom in for a close-up when you think you have found something interesting.

All this has shaped my way of working, of conceiving projects, and has also influenced my approach to fashion. That approach has been gradual precisely because the constant movement of my subject impelled me to continually adjust my focus and required me to exchange views with others and to find people who would help me meet the challenge of putting fashion under the spotlight, seeking to present a comprehensive picture of its relationship with the world (as happens, for example, with the various designers covered in the *Mode* series;[2] as has happened for this book, and not just this book, with Angelo Flaccavento; as happens in my role as director of the degree course in Fashion Design at the IUAV in Venice). I feel the need to make clearer this concept, which is less philological than it might appear. My effort to convey a full picture of the relationship between fashion and the world always implies the possibility of putting together a different account and offering new perspectives on fashion. Thus mine is not an attempt at historical fidelity to fashion, but a critical exercise that I believe is part of the process of fashion, in other words of fashion in its becoming. I am also fascinated by the relations that fashion has with other disciplines, by the way that an item of clothing, a fashion photograph, a photographic feature can immediately put us in touch with the dreams, the obsessions and the shifts in a culture and a society.

I am attracted by the forceful flow of images rather than by the wonder of forms. Succeeding in grasping in the succession of images that one fragment, that figure, that clue which will allow you (and Cayce Pollard, the protagonist of William Gibson's novel *Pattern Recognition*,[3] springs to mind here) to verify an intuition, an idea, and to imagine a history, is for me the equivalent of the joy of the water diviner when the feels the rod move in his hands. From this point of view, my way of working is perhaps better suited to research in the sphere of fashion (for instance in the processes of identification of trends and style directions) than to academic research. Nothing is more remote than the present and at the same time there is nothing closer. It appears to us as a landscape

[2]   The *Mode* series, which I have been directing for almost six years, is a project of the Fondazione Pitti Discovery and Marsilio Editori devoted to the ideas and figures of fashion. The most recent title, edited in collaboration with Stefano Tonchi, is *Walter Albini and His Times. All Power to the Imagination* (2010), a book that, functioning almost as an exhibition, uses the figure of this visionary Italian fashion designer to carry out an important reflection on the decade that saw the affirmation of fashion as a fundamental element in the representation of contemporaneity and the definitive shift away from the atelier that permitted the success of Italian ready-to-wear.
[3]   William Gibson, *Pattern Recognition*. New York: G.P. Putnam's Sons, 2003.

that is changing continually under our eyes, lacking the architectural structure that past eras seem to possess. A phantasmagoria of bright lights and deep shadows.

For some time now I have begun to concentrate in a more systematic way on the Italian culture of fashion. At this moment I feel a strong need to work on the roots and on the future of Italian fashion, since there are shortcomings and gaps that I would like to help to overcome. And while I have already made some moves in this direction,[4] it seems to me that the work has just begun. I feel an urgent necessity to tackle it from the perspective with which I feel most comfortable, that of the curator, capable of observing the unfolding of time as past and present at once. A time amalgamated by strong contrasts, based on the accumulation of information and on easy access to the data. In a dimension that is current as well as one that takes a long view. The challenge, however, is the present, which appears to us as a kaleidoscopic image with a thousand facets. The last books to have been published in our country as activist accounts, directly engaged with their subject, were the ones that came out during the boom in the phenomenon of Italian fashion in the eighties, or immediately beforehand, in an attempt to convey its depth and importance.

"The ambition of this work is twofold: to present the public with an informative cross section of the world of Italian fashion; and to offer the protagonists of this world a critical contribution on their activity, setting aside the laudatory tradition of journalism specializing in the sector. We have moved in this direction because we are convinced that the vital importance of the fashion industry on the economic plane should be accompanied by a cultural awareness that currently appears absent." This is what Silvia Giacomoni wrote in 1983 in the preface to her book *L'Italia della Moda*, drawing attention even then, at that truly exciting time, to the existence of several structural defects. But earlier still, in 1979, Adriana Mulassano had published her book *I Mass Moda. Fatti e personaggi dell'italian look* (her companion in this adventure, as in Giacomoni's, was the photographer Alfa Castaldi), which set out to reconstruct the stages in the development of Italian fashion from 1951 until the seminal years for the definition of ready-to-wear through an examination of forty leading figures in the country's fashion and textile industries. The volume also includes a section devoted to a sort of press review of the period, entitled "What did the Newspapers Say?" The last press cutting is an article signed by Natalia Aspesi and published in *La Repubblica* on March 23, 1976: "Buying clothes seems to have become the last refuge from anxiety and insecurity; making clothes is the great hope of our industry in crisis. Selling clothes abroad is a sure way of covering much of the billions spent on importing oil [...]. In Milan from morning to evening is staged the grand ritual of prestigious fashion, which is no longer that of the great couturiers but that of the small and medium-sized luxury

[4]   I am thinking of the exhibition and book projects I have carried out first with Pitti Immagine and then with the Fondazione Pitti Discovery. Among these it is worth mentioning *Uniform: Order And Disorder* (Florence-New York 2001), *Total Living* (Milan 2003), *Excess: Fashion and the Underground in the 80s* (Florence 2004), *Italian Eyes: Italian Fashion Photography from 1951 to Today* (Milan 2005), *Human Game: Winners And Losers* (Florence 2006) and *Simonetta: The First Lady of Italian Fashion* (Florence 2008).

industries which have managed to persuade the whole world that dressing Italian style is a mark of intelligence, taste and being up-to-date."

Pia Soli's *Il genio antipatico. Creatività e tecnologia della moda italiana 1951-1983* dates instead from 1984 and is the catalogue of the exhibition of the same name held in April-May of that year in the Salone dei Congressi of the car park at the Galoppatoio of Villa Borghese in Rome. In the introduction to this book made up mostly of pictures–many of them, forming an extraordinary repertoire–the author wrote: "Fashion sits very well with the Italian character because it is individualistic and capable of seeing solutions that are always different and unique [...]. This still indomitable individuality has served to spread fashion in a fantastic way all over the country: the Italy of added value, the Italy of export, capable of absorbing everything and spitting it out again in a different form in a very short space of time."

I have chosen to quote from these books, but there are many others that have examined, and tried to describe and explain from different angles, a manufacturing, cultural and economic phenomenon that has certainly revolutionized the image of Italy in the world. It is likely that this necessary intensity was the product of years spent in self-examination and in feeling part of a group, of a movement that represented a break with the past, but also a constructive and trailblazing force. Just think of the artists lumped together under highly successful labels–arte povera, transavanguardia, nuovi-nuovi, to cite the most incisive examples–invented by the critics and fellow travelers Germano Celant, Achille Bonito Oliva and Renato Barilli. They interpreted the anxieties and dreams of the world. Their images revealed worlds and words found the reasons for these worlds. There is an image that epitomizes that moment and the attention which Italy enjoyed: it is on the cover of the catalogue of the exhibition *Identité Italienne* at the Centre Pompidou in Paris (1981), a history of Italian art since 1959 recounted in the grainy black-and-white of those years. A boundless galaxy in which the works mingle to form new constellations.

But it is in no way my intention to dream of the past: each time has its own rhythm and fashion is the discipline that is able to mold the forms of time on each occasion that it inhabits them. Indeed I would like to leave that history in the background and use it only as a device of passage. None of us wishes to keep still and even less do we want to go backward. We are linked sentimentally to the past that has shaped us, but we are also eager to move on to the future that awaits us. To set yourself the promotion of the Italian fashion of the younger generations as an objective does not signify defending its borders, its national identity in a reactionary way, and still less holding up a new world in contrast to the recent past. Rather it is a question of comprehending contemporary fashion, the one that is still in progress, as it is being shaped and tested in our country. It means promoting our artistic language without turning it into a nationalistic flag. The aim of the cultural operation that underpins this book is to identify the current generation of Italian fashion designers, characterized by a new and different way of working. It allows us to describe them and perhaps even to define them. Or rather, to define the specific role that they play on the international scene of contemporary fashion. The world of Italian fashion is still associated with terms like sarto or stilista[5] that are now obsolete, and there are probably two reasons for this, both of which are our own responsibility: on the one hand the difficulty we have in reflecting on the past and on our history, on the other our inability to risk an interpretation of the present that would allow us to outline future scenarios. The systematic attempt to take a new look at the history of Italian fashion in the 20th century through a reflection capable, for example, of examining what was going on in Italy in the twenties and thirties is surprisingly recent. And this delay, along with a general unwillingness to project ourselves consciously into the future, explains for instance why we are still so haunted and constrained by a label, that of stilista, which seems to have become a timeless condition, but which is instead strongly linked to a precise historical moment, the one spanning two decades, the seventies and the eighties, that saw the international success of "Made in Italy." Even this last phenomenon must be treated today as a system of creation and production that needs to be redefined and reinterpreted. It is probably an outdated system, as was suggested by Miuccia Prada herself when in 2010 she launched the capsule collection "Made In," an ironic reference to the impossibility of laying claim today to an Italian authenticity on the basis of the provenance of the materials and the production, seeking instead to bring everything back to the concept and, more in general, to then quality of the fashion design carried out by the brand.

It is by adopting this perspective that we can try to speak of an Italian fashion design and of a new generation of designers who are no longer just either sarti or stilisti, but who, whether working for a brand that is not their own or devoting themselves to a personal project, operate with a flexible attitude that implies at one and the same time a technical and sartorial know-how and the visionary capacity that is a fundamental quality of the figure of the creative director.

From sarto to stilista, and no further: the history of Italian fashion, even today, seems to recognize only the movements that take us directly from the fifties to the eighties.[6] Then it bogs down, grinds to a halt, in the sense that from the nineties onward no attempt was made to focus on the specific nature of Italian fashion. It is on the contrary absolutely necessary for us to pause and reflect on what has happened in Italy, on what has happened since the nineties, since the decade that brought the 20th century to a close and during which the figure of the creative director burst onto the scene. This development has led to a very interesting modification of equilibria that has shifted the Italian dimension from the creativity of the individual to the brand (and to the history of the brand for which we now use the English word heritage). Gucci has been the most emblematic Italian case: we cannot fail to mention the creative director par excellence, Tom Ford, who in partnership with Domenico De Sole, the CEO and for years

---

[5] The terms, which literally mean "tailor" or "dressmaker" and "stylist" respectively, are used in Italian as rough equivalents of "couturier" and "fashion designer," but with the cultural baggage referred to in the text by the author. Translator's note.
[6] And perhaps so does the "Italian history" of fashion: shifting the adjective allows us to highlight the fact that the problem which we are discussing stems in part from a certain tardiness in developing a specifically Italian current of fashion studies in academic circles, a delay for which attempts to compensate have been made in recent years.

the real company man, relaunched the brand globally in the second half of the nineties, a legacy then taken up by the very Italian Frida Giannini with surprising results. While the companies remained Italian in their tradition and in the collective imagination, the visionaries at the helm of the brands came from abroad.[7] Even without seeking direct motivations that would run the risk of being over-simplistic, it is hard not to link this fact with the prolonged lack in Italy of the right investment in training in the field of fashion design: the designers who have emerged since the eighties have continued to act as stilisti, sometimes bolstering their mythology in a decidedly anachronistic manner, and no institution has taken the trouble to develop means of capitalizing on the specific characteristics of the Italian situation and turning them into a genuine system of cultural reflection and academic education in the field of fashion. Today the need for change is reflected primarily through an institutional response that finds expression in the attempt to introduce fashion among the disciplines taught in universities.[8] Simultaneously identifying and bringing together the people who we are presenting in this publication is a first, partial, but decidedly necessary step toward analysis and interpretation of the situation in Italy. They make up a heterogeneous group of designers who operate in different ways. Some of them are reviving an approach close to craftsmanship with its roots in tailoring, which often looks back to a past whose memory is reappropriated through exploration of the archives. They are constantly seeking to translate this craftsmanship, to compare it with and relate it to Italian industry, which is not just that of the clothing companies, but also the textile manufacturers. These Italian talents, unlike the ones who came out of the schools of the United Kingdom or Belgium and who dominated the second half of the nineties, do not reflect on fashion design in an abstract (and purely concept-oriented) way, but try to bring out and give form to a personal interpretation of fashion by cross-fertilizing the techniques of couture with the dimension of industry (the industry, in turn, is growing increasingly conscious of the fact that these new designers are a source of research and innovation, and offer the possibility of a fundamental encounter). The return to the individual (which allows us to speak once again not only of great Italian brands, but of talents too) is interesting as it shows that the problem is no longer simply that of giving someone the label of couturier or fashion designer, but of recognizing that the new talents move between these extremes, always keeping their eyes focused on research

[7]   In this connection, we must also point out the case of Emilio Pucci: since 2000 the brand has been part of the French luxury-goods conglomerate LVMH run by Bernard Arnault, which owns a 67% stake. Laudomia Pucci, Emilio's daughter and until 2000 designer for the brand (from 1998 to 2000 with Stephan Janson), became image director, while the LVMH group appointed as creative directors first Julio Espada (2000-02) and Christian Lacroix (2002-05), and then Matthew Williamson (2005-08) and Peter Dundas (in the post since 2008).

[8]   At the IUAV University in Venice we are obtaining excellent results in the area of the training of the fashion designer. For six years in fact we have been running a degree course in Fashion Design, of which I am the director. After following the curriculum for three years our students present a project for a final collection that they realize in its entirety, thereby demonstrating that they have acquired a new kind of hands-on know-how, which they are constantly stimulated to confront and cross-fertilize with the specifics of the company dimension, a goal that is guaranteed by important relations of collaboration that the degree course has established with some of the major Italian fashion houses. Since last year we have added to the curriculum a master's degree course in Fashion Design and Theory, which promotes a critical reflection on fashion supported by advanced workshops of fashion design. Several other Italian universities have introduced courses in the field of fashion, in particular Milan Polytechnic, which has also introduced a design-oriented three-year degree course and master's degree course.

and on industrial production, as well as making constant reference to the Italian tradition.

Obviously not everyone occupies the same position in this panorama. We find figures who deal more directly with the identity of a brand and its products, tending to hybridize and personalize it through a vision that embraces its history and the sensibility of the designer; others, instead, can be considered more experimental and independent[9] as they seek to develop and configure new ways of working with industry, thereby helping to redefine it and bring its procedures and time frames up to date; then there are those who move in a world that can almost be described as haute couture but which survives today precisely because it does not ignore the problems of industrial production and technology, which in these more experimental examples seem really to be the horizon and the means of keeping high fashion alive (and it almost seems possible to hypothesize an approach that could be called techno-couture and that would undermine the traditional seasonal organization with new schedules for fashion or rather for the fashion system).

II

WITH US FASHION DID NOT COME OUT OF THE AVANT-GARDE, BUT OUT OF AN ANCIENT AND WIDESPREAD FABRIC OF MANUFACTURING AND CRAFTSMANSHIP. IT HAS HAD TO CONFRONT A MODERN, CHAOTIC AND HOSTILE WORLD, TO FIGHT TO SURVIVE. ITALIAN FASHION WAS NOT BORN AS SPECTACLE, PROVOCATION, PURE AMUSEMENT. BURT AS AN INDUSTRY THAT SET OUT TO MAKE ITSELF USEFUL, TO DRESS PEOPLE. IT DID NOT WANT TO UNDERMINE IDENTITIES, BUT TO GIVE THEM BACK.

(Francesco Alberoni)

MEMORY IS A MARVELOUS THING. BUT A PERSON WHO CANNOT FORGET IS IN DEEP TROUBLE. REMEMBERING AND FORGETTING ARE BOTH IMPORTANT.

(Joseph Beuys)

All the designers covered in this volume have come to the fore as authors, as protagonists, either with their own lines or as creative directors since 2000, and many of them after the first half of the decade that has just come to an end. Some of them have had to "translate other languages," as Giambattista Valli put it very succinctly in an old interview,[10] before winning their independence; others have become the creative directors of important national and international brands, doing very well and

---

8   With the label "independent" the intent is not so much to define an alternative position with respect to the production and commercial system tout court, as to characterize the kind of fashion design that does not conform to mainstream aesthetics constructed around consumers identified by marketing-oriented strategies or to the constraints of official calendars, precisely because they try to find niches of independence where clothing and accessories become a space of research and a means of presenting possible alternative scenarios, shaped by unprecedented formal and conceptual combinations.

10   "I've been a translator of other languages for many years. I've been a chameleon. I've had many experiences in large groups. Very important experiences that I recommend to all young potential designers. But the day comes when you want the freedom to speak your own language and you want to speak it in total independence" (Maria Luisa Frisa, "Sogno Italiano," in *L'Espresso*, n. 2, 15 January 2009).

succeeding in the most difficult challenge of all, that of reconciling the origins and the tradition of a brand with the need to put yourself on the line and obtaining results that show it is possible to innovate even from within strictly imposed limits; others have decided, often finding companies to act as their willing partners, to produce their own clothes with small independent projects and have used competitions and prizes as a showcase for their work;[11] yet others have chosen to turn themselves into creative workshops supplying ideas and designs to brands in need of renewal.

Relating to them and their stories, trying to understand their work, has obliged me to reckon with the history of Italian fashion over the last thirty years, and not just that of fashion. Art, literature, industrial design, architecture and the cinema have contributed with their images to giving value to actions and gestures; just as the political vicissitudes of our country have been fundamental for me in filling out the background to people and objects. Even though, unfortunately, as Enrico Deaglio writes in the introduction to his book *Patria* "[...] there is little kiss kiss and a lot of bang bang."[12]

To get my bearings in the definition of an intentionally unstable geography of the Italian fashion of the younger generations–seeking to establish a dialogue between very different personalities and events–I have felt the need to grasp what have really been the generational passages, the missed opportunities and the silences, and why something has got stuck since the eighties. A very Italian and very Milanese stereotype identifies fashion with ready-to-wear and the eighties. This happens because Italy, in that decade, invented and launched the cult of the fashion designer. It was a great revolution in the history and the culture of fashion that changed ideas and practices of consumption at an international level. The production and cultural model of ready-to-wear is still sound, obviously, but is losing its dominant position and capacity to interpret the spirit of the time. It is for this reason that continuing to think it is the only model or even the strongest stops us not only from looking forward, but also from deciphering what is new.

I I I

WHAT CAN I DO WITH WHAT I FIND?
(Nicolas Bourriand)

For the younger generations the years of Made in Italy and of Milan's celebrated nightlife are very far away. They have read Bret Easton Ellis's *Lunar Park* and now his *Imperial Bedrooms*, but are not interested in his *American Psycho*. Perhaps some of

---

[11] One of the most important of these competitions is undoubtedly *Who's on Next*. Intended to "scout new generations of fashion designers" and promoted by Altaroma and Vogue Italia, it has been giving awards to Italian designers or foreign ones resident in Italy since 2005 and has seen many of the designers featured in this book play a leading role, including Albino, Aquilano e Rimondi, Sara Lanzi, Isabella Tonchi, Gabriele Colangelo, Marco De Vincenzo and Leitmotiv. Since 2009 *Who's on Next* Uomo, devoted to designers of menswear (both clothing and accessories), has also been staged, in collaboration with Pitti Immagine, and on the second occasion was won by Fabio Quaranta. In 2011 this was joined by *Who's on Next* Bimbo, again in collaboration with Pitti Immagine and devoted to fashion for children. It is also worth mentioning *ITS International Talents Support*, the competition held in Trieste that pits fashion schools from all over the world and their best students against one another.

[12] Enrico Deaglio, *Patria 1978-2008*. Milan: Il Saggiatore, 2009.

them are old enough to be familiar with the novels of Pier Vittorio Tondelli, but those atmospheres and emotions are too blurred. They prefer to stay in the present: they are fascinated by the ambiance of Luca Guadagnino's movie *I Am Love*, which paints a picture of a haute bourgeois, elegant Italy, but one in which the elegance is restrained and based on values of quality. It is no accident that the textile manufacturers who are the protagonists of the film display all the traits of that family solidity which has been the foundation of the success of Italian fashion in the world. Or they choose to go back to the origins find a new identity: to Walter Albini, the restless dreamer, precursor of ready-to-wear, but also to the sartorial magic that was put on show in the Sala Bianca at Palazzo Pitti, abandoned en masse in the seventies as it was seen as elitist and antiquated by the generation of great designers who went on to build the image of Milan as the city of fashion. Or, again, they like to rummage in the sophisticated atmospheres of the Rome of *La Dolce Vita* where fashion was interwoven with the cinema, art and literature in an extraordinary cosmopolitan mix kneaded out of "free and gratuitous creativity," as Paola Pitagora puts it in her *Fiato d'artista*[13] published by Sellerio. Aware of living in the age of postproduction, they sample forms and fragments and then present them in a different context.

Some have studied architecture, providing confirmation of an attitude toward design that is founded on the conception of the garment as the result of a planned and conscious intervention in its forms. Others have studied humanities or perhaps the history of art at university or followed the DAMS course or attended the Academy of Fine Arts. But the majority have been to fashion schools in Italy and abroad. In them we can recognize those new citizens of the world that have been produced by the supremacy of the fashion mentality. Individuals without prejudices, flexible, with an open personality and tastes that are in continual evolution. "In the empire of fashion what amounts to the cultural power of novelty requires special emphasis. Class rivalry is insignificant compared to the effects of the social signification that single-handedly generates the taste for difference, that precipitates boredom with anything repetitive, that makes people love and want anything that changes, almost before the fact," writes the philosopher Gilles Lipovetsky.[14] *This Is Tomorrow* was the title of a mythical exhibition staged in London in the fifties that changed our way of looking at the future by mixing together art, architecture, photography, graphic design and fashion, all under the banner of pop art. The new protagonists of fashion have taken the lesson on board and hop without inhibitions from one discipline to another, picking out practices and methods.

During the nineties the majority of them were receiving their education and training in the profession, while the fashion system was growing more complex and becoming consolidated, incorporating all the weaknesses and contradictions that were emerging and turning into that voracious "total living" put forward by labels and definitions of fashion as industry and cultural form.[15] In the design of an ever more sophisticated reality,

[13] Paola Pitagora, *Fiato d'artista. Dieci anni a Piazza del Popolo*, Palermo: Sellerio, 2001.
[14] Gilles Lipovetsky, *L'Empire de l'éphémère, la mode et son destin dans les sociétés modernes*, Paris: Gallimard, 1987.
[15] Maria Luisa Frisa, Mario Lupano and Stefano Tonchi (eds.), *Total Living*. Milan: Charta, 2002.

determined to promote precise lifestyles in which habits, spaces and even atmospheres made up a varied catalogue on which anyone could draw to create him or herself a character and find a role in the global entertainment of fashion. A strange and uneven decade, comprised between the rubble left by the collapse of the Berlin Wall in 1989 and that of the attack on the Twin Towers in 2001. Marked by the realization that AIDS was a disease which had to be reckoned with on a daily basis. In Italy: the passage from the First to the Second Republic, the beginning of the Berlusconi era that has perverted the dreams and desires, the rights and duties of an entire nation, leaving the task of molding behavior and morality in the hands of television and the strategy of gossip.

In the books on Italian fashion of those years, with the exclusion of the protagonists (Gucci signed Tom Ford and Prada), little information is to be found: no text devoted to the history of fashion wormed its way into the recesses of this decade until 2000.[16] What traces have been preserved are largely in some magazines and on the web. And yet there were eccentric and seminal experiences in this period that saw the triumph of the caustic, elusive and subtly underground figure codified by Raf Simons in *The Fourth Sex*, an exploration to the notes of Kurt Cobain's *Smells Like Teen Spirit* of that rebellious, icy and no-future youth which Hedi Slimane was to transform into a sartorial and androgynous figure. The attention shifted to other territories, toward fashion that broke the rules, distorted the forms and entered on a collision course with the body. A body that, in the photographs of Juergen Teller and Corinne Day, exhibited its new reality based on rejection and intolerance of the rules of the game. So as soon as bodies contracted, abandoning the lavish curves of Wonder Woman, it was Prada that dominated, using "technical" nylon for clothes that introduced a new concept of beauty. It was one side of the minimalist aesthetic that redefined bodies and attitudes and of which Helmut Lang remains the most often cited exponent. And in 1996 Amy Spindler placed Ennio Capasa alongside Helmut Lang: "His style has influenced heavyweight labels like Calvin Klein and Gucci. He, along with Helmut Lang, is most often credited for inventing the mood of men's fashion for the 1990s, much as Giorgio Armani did for the 80s."[17]

Capasa was one of the Italian protagonists of the decade. As were Antonio Marras[18] and Maurizio Altieri of Carpe Diem, two designers who epitomize the need to preserve a language of your own and a difference by keeping at a distance from the center. Carpe Diem is an experience that has now come to an end but one that left an indelible mark, still evident in the use of fine materials immediately brought into confrontation with the time, in the refusal to submit to the constraints of the seasons of the fashion calendar and in those stores which underline the material character of clothing by hanging it from butcher's hooks (which are anyway used by patternmakers). An eccentric experience like that of Marras, currently creative director of Kenzo as well and a designer capable of

[16] "The point is always the same, where there is not a present that takes it upon oneself. The past never becomes history. The tiger's leap is missing. The Tigersprung so often invoked by the theory of fashion. So that the analysis of this lack could be one of the fundamental themes for fashion studies in Italy today," writes Paola Colaiacomo in her introduction to *Fatto in Italia. La cultura del made in Italy (1960-2000)*. Rome: Meltemi, 2006.
[17] Amy M. Spindler, "Fault Line of a New Generation," in *The New York Times*, December 17, 1996.
[18] Antonio Mancinelli, *Antonio Marras*, Venezia-Firenze, Marsilio-Fondazione Pitti Discovery, 2009.

taking the imagery of his birthplace Sardinia out of its context, reassembling it out of sync and proposing a fashion that is continually put to the test by error. Both have made moves in the same direction, aiming to define a territory where it is possible to construct an alternative that is not antagonistic but complementary.

I V

IMAGINATION IS THE FIRST, LAST AND MOST IMPORTANT PLACE FOR A WORK OF ART.
(Gabriel Orozco)

The absence of a reflection on the recent evolution of Italian fashion can also be blamed on a lack of curators capable of identifying the new creative forces and of developing a critical discourse on the poetics of Italian fashion design. Once again this is an effect of our delay with regard to academic training in the field, a tardiness that has prevented us from undertaking operations like the one carried out by Bronwyn Cosgrave in 2005: *Sample*[19] was in fact a survey that entrusted to each of the ten curators invited to take part (they included editors, designers, stylists and writers) the task of picking ten new fashion designers in order to present a picture of global fashion from many different perspectives. Even though Milan was numbered among the cities in which to look for designers, no Italian curator appeared in the book[20] (and the only Italian designer was Giambattista Valli) to point out the specific features of our fashion that it would be hard for anyone else to promote and that we cannot go on reducing solely and exclusively to the catwalks of Milan. This is another of the central elements on which this publication seeks to reflect, as it aims to show how the current situation in Italy is bringing decidedly into question the city's supposed role as the center of the country's fashion: it is a dispersed manifesto that seeks out and draws attention to a wide range of voices and places, which are crying out in fact to be seen as part of a system and not simply boiled down to a single poetics or a single capital.[21] The absence of authoritative critical voices has left the job of identifying the "latest innovations" in fashion for too long to young fashionista bloggers: this has helped to maintain and impose a reductive vision of fashion design, without encouraging the development of a more profound reflection on contemporary Italian fashion, which must instead succeed in earning itself a place in the international limelight, without complexes, on a par with the other countries that have made the promotion of creative people a formidable machine of territorial marketing. This publishing project is a step in this direction: it represents a first attempt to identify with a critical and selective gaze the new breeding grounds of talents, the new centers of

[19] Bronwyn Cosgrave (ed.), *Sample: 100 Fashion Designers—010 Curators—Cuttings from Contemporary Fashion*. London: Phaidon, 2005.
[20] The ten curators were Tim Blanks, Patricia Carta, Ulrich Lehmann, Alexander McQueen, Arianne Phillips, Harriet Quick, Stephen Todd, Kyoichi Tsuzuki, Walter Van Beirendonck and Brana Wolf.
[21] Of the designers examined in this book Stefano Pilati, Riccardo Tisci and Giambattista Valli work in Paris; Frida Giannini, Maria Grazia Chiuri and Pier Paolo Piccioli, Sergio Zambon, Marco De Vincenzo and Fabio Quaranta in Rome; Sara Lanzi and Mariavittoria Sargentini in Perugia; Boboutic and Massimiliano Giornetti in Florence; Leitmotiv in Bologna; Franco Verzi in Riccione. Vincenzo De Cotiis, Renato Montagner, Carlo Contrada and Alessandro Sartori lead a nomadic existence between the places where they live and work and the centers of production. All of the other designers work in Milan.

production and, above all, the galaxy of designers who are offering a kaleidoscopic, but also a rigorous vision of the new Italian fashion. In seeking to take stock of this melting pot of voices, an attempt has been made to explore an unstable geography and to interpret it through passages and collisions between not just the languages of fashion, but other languages as well, in those zones of transition where the different disciplines find points of contact and reveal (and this especially true of fashion) the here and now of our time. Fashion lives in relationship with other systems, and is open to being shaken up and inspired by everything that is extraneous to it, not just in forms and modes but also in values and aims. There is no question that the scene this book tries to map out will have omissions that may be considered extremely grave by many, as it will include figures that others will regard as unwarranted, but the intention was not to carry out a census or draw up a list. We are speaking of a situation in flux, complicated to picture, to bring into focus, to pin down in a reliable and systematic way. Rather, the intention is to present a point of view, to propose a critical selection, with a willingness to take risks in order to draw attention to a group of designers whose work not only reflects their own poetics, but also, through their choices and personal creative strategies, the changes in the way the work of fashion design is done in relation to a complex and powerful system that has by now spread all over the world. It would be a fine thing if this project were to give rise to other proposals, other books; if it were to succeed in outlining other pulsating constellations in the multifaceted galaxy of Italian contemporary fashion.

To Angelo and to Mario. Thanks and many thanks to Judith Clark, Riccardo Dirindin, Gabriele Monti

ESSENTIAL BIBLIOGRAPHICAL REFERENCES

Amendola, Eva Paola (ed.), *Vestire italiano. Quarant'anni di moda nelle immagini dei grandi fotografi*. Rome: Oberon, 1983

Belfanti, Carlo Marco; Giusberti, Fabio (eds.), *Storia d'Italia. Annali 19. La moda*. Turin: Einaudi, 2003

Bianchino, Gloria; Butazzi, Grazietta; Mottola Molfino, Alessandra; Quintavalle, Arturo Carlo (eds.), *La moda italiana. Le origini dell'Alta Moda e la maglieria*. Milan: Electa, 1987

Bianchino, Gloria; Quintavalle, Arturo Carlo, *Moda. Dalla fiaba al design. Italia 1951-1989*. Novara: De Agostini, 1989

Bocca, Nicoletta (ed.), *Moda. Poesia e progetto. Percorsi della creatività*. Milan: Domus Academy, 1990

Bottero, Amelia, *Nostra signora la moda*. Milan: Mursia, 1979

Butazzi, Grazietta; Mottola Molfino, Alessandra (ed.), *La moda italiana. Dall'antimoda allo stilismo*, Milan, Electa, 1987

Centro Italiano per lo Studio della Storia del Tessuto (ed.), *Per una storia della moda pronta. Problemi e ricerche*, proceedings of the 5th International Conference of the CISST (Milan, February 26-28, 1990). Florence: Edifir, 1991

Colaiacomo, Paola (ed.), *Fatto in Italia. La cultura del made in Italy (1960-2000)*. Rome: Meltemi, 2006

Colaiacomo, Paola; Frisa, Maria Luisa, "Some Random Notes on Italian Fashion. The Fashion of Postmodernism," in Durland Spilker, Kaye; Sadako Takeda, Sharon, *Breaking the Mode: Contemporary Fashion from the Permanent Collection of the Los Angeles Museum of Art*, catalogue of the exhibition *Contromoda. La moda contemporanea della collezione permanente del Los Angeles County Museum of Art* at Palazzo Strozzi, Florence, October 12, 2007-January 20, 2008). Milan: Skira, 2007

D'Amato, Gabriella, *Moda e design. Stili e accessori del Novecento*. Milan: Bruno Mondadori, 2007

Fortunati, Leopoldina; Danese, Elda (eds.), *Manuale di comunicazione, sociologia e cultura della moda*. Vol. 3, *Il made in Italy*. Rome: Meltemi, 2005

Frisa, Maria Luisa (ed.), *Gianfranco Ferré. Lessons in Fashion*, Venice-Florence, Marsilio-Fondazione Pitti Discovery, 2009

Frisa, Maria Luisa (ed.), *Lo sguardo italiano. Fotografie italiane di moda dal 1951 a oggi*, with Francesco Bonami and Anna Mattirolo, catalogue of the exhibition at the Rotonda di Via Besana, Milan, February 25-March 20, 2005. Milan-Florence: Charta-Fondazione Pitti Discovery, 2005

Frisa, Maria Luisa, "Today's Muse. At the origins of an Italian style in fashion," in Caratozzolo, Vittoria Caterina; Clark, Judith; Frisa, Maria Luisa, *Simonetta : The First Lady of Italian Fashion*, published to coincide with the exhibition *Simonetta. La prima donna della moda italiana* at the Galleria del Costume di Palazzo Pitti, Florence, January 9-February 17, 2008). Venice-Florence: Marsilio-Fondazione Pitti Discovery, 2008

Frisa, Maria Luisa; Tonchi, Stefano (ed.), *Walter Albini and His Time. All Power to the Imagination*. Venice-Florence: Marsilio-Fondazione Pitti Discovery, 2010

Gastel, Minnie, *Cinquant'anni di moda italiana. Breve storia del prêt-à-porter*. Milan: Vallardi, 1995

Giacomoni, Silvia, *L'Italia della moda*, photographs by Alfa Castaldi. Milan: Mazzotta, 1984

Giordani Aragno, Bonizza (ed.), *La Sardegna veste la moda*, catalogue of the exhibition at the Galleria del Costume di Palazzo Pitti, Florence, June 17-July 16, 2009)., Sassari: C. Delfino, 2009

Giordani Aragno, Bonizza (ed.), *Moda Italia. Creativity and technology in the Italian fashion system / Creatività, impresa, tecnologia nel sistema italiano della moda*, graphic design by Italo Lupi, catalogue of the exhibition at Pier 88, New York, April 1988). Milan: Domus, 1988

Gnoli, Sofia, *Un secolo di moda italiana 1900-2000*. Rome: Meltemi, 2005

Merlo, Elisabetta, *Moda italiana. Storia di un'industria dall'Ottocento a oggi*. Venice: Marsilio, 2008[2]

Morini, Enrica, "Gli stilisti," in Calabrese, Omar (ed.), *Il modello italiano. Forme della creatività*. Milan: Skira, 1998. English ed., *Italian Style: Forms of Creativity*. Milan: Skira, 1999

Morini, Enrica, *Storia della Moda XVIII-XX secolo*. Milan: Skira, 2000

Mulassano, Adriana, *I Mass Moda. Fatti e personaggi dell'Italian look*. Milan: G. Spinelli & C., 1979

Paris, Ivan, *Oggetti cuciti. L'abbigliamento pronto in Italia dal primo dopoguerra agli anni Settanta*. Milan: Franco Angeli, 2006

Segre Reinach, Simona, "La moda nella cultura italiana," in Petrini, Carlo; Volli, Ugo (eds.), *La cultura italiana*. Vol. VI, *Cibo, gioco, festa, moda*. Turin: UTET, 2009

Segre Reinach, Simona, "Milan as a Fashion City," in Eicher, Joanne (ed.), *The Encyclopedia of World Dress and Fashion*. Oxford-New York: Berg, 2010

Soli, Pia, *Il genio antipatico. Creatività e tecnologia della moda italiana 1951-1983*, catalogue of the exhibition at the Salone dei Congressi del Parcheggio al Galoppatoio di Villa Borghese, Rome, April-May 1984). Milan: Mondadori, 1984

Steele, Valerie, *Fashion, Italian Style*. New Haven-London: Yale University Press, 2003

Steele, Valerie; Carrara, Gillion, "Italian Fashion," in Steele, Valerie (ed.), *Encyclopedia of Clothing and Fashion*. Detroit: Charles Scribner's Sons, 2005

Vaccari, Alessandra, *Il Made in Italy nell'epoca della postproduzione*, in Muzzarelli, Maria Giuseppina; Riello, Giorgio; Tosi Brandi, Elisa (eds.), *Moda. Storia e Storie*. Milan: Bruno Mondadori, 2010

Vergani, Guido (ed.), *Dizionario della moda* (2010 edition). Milan: Baldini Castoldi Dalai, 2009

White, Nicola, *Reconstructing Italian Fashion. America and the development of the Italian fashion industry*. Oxford-New York: Berg, 2000

tracks

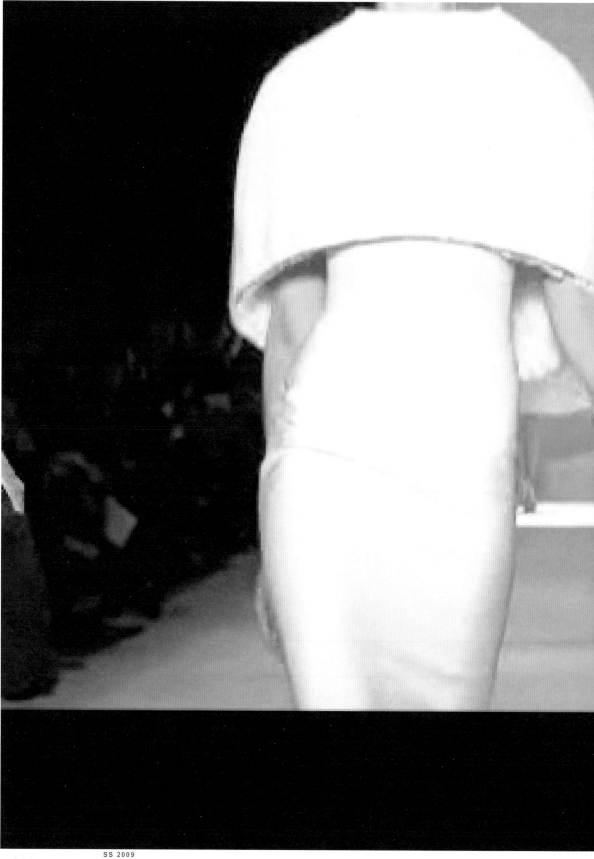

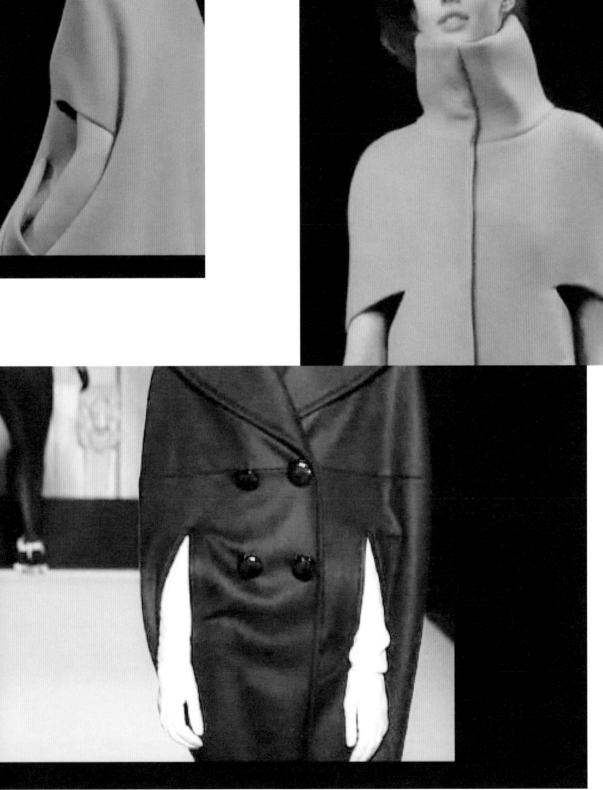

SS 2011

YSL, FW 2008-2009   YSL, FW 2008-2009

YSL, SS 2010

YSL, SS 2010

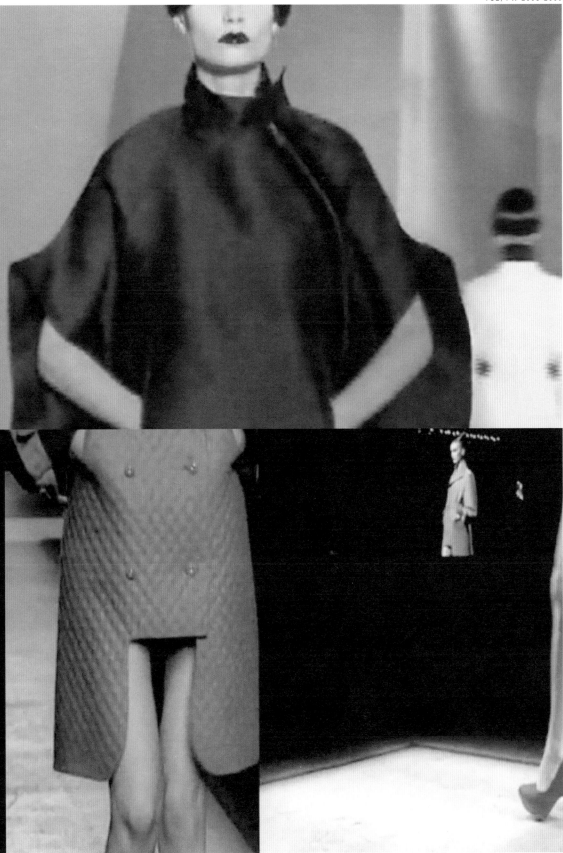

MILA SCHÖN, FW 2010-2011

MILA SCHÖN, FW 2010-2011

MILA SCHÖN, SS 2010

MILA SCHÖN, SS 2010

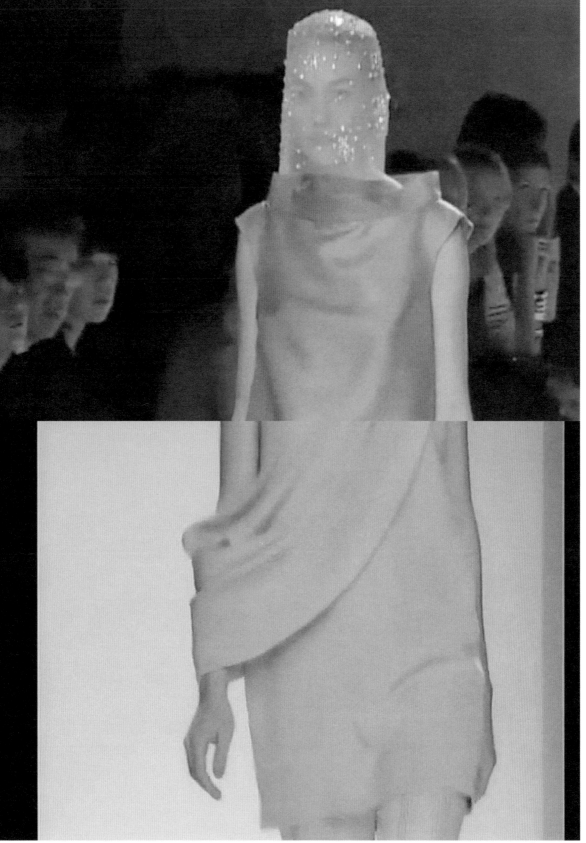

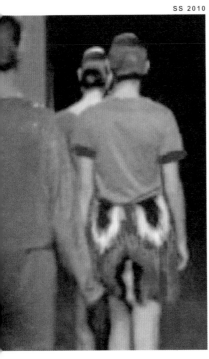

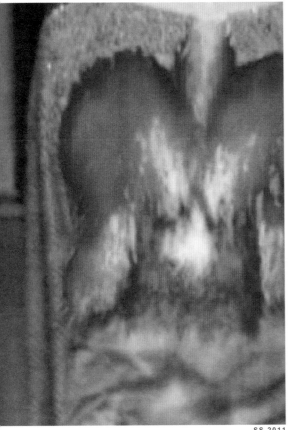

FW 2010-2011

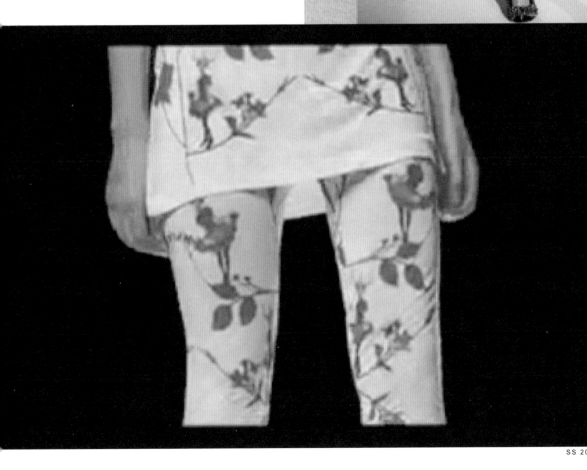

GUCCI, SS 2010

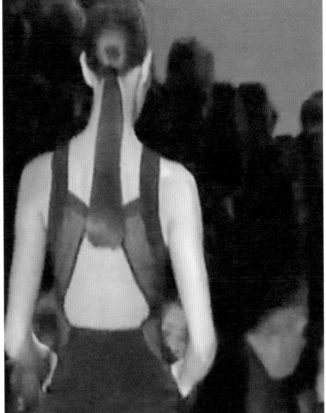

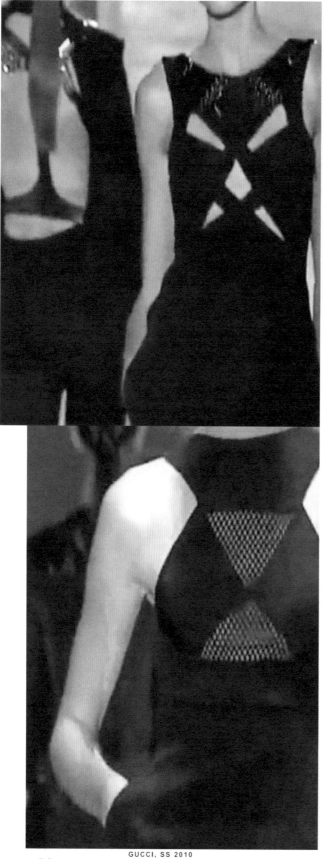

GUCCI, SS 2010

56

GUCCI, FW 2006-2007

GUCCI, SS 2011

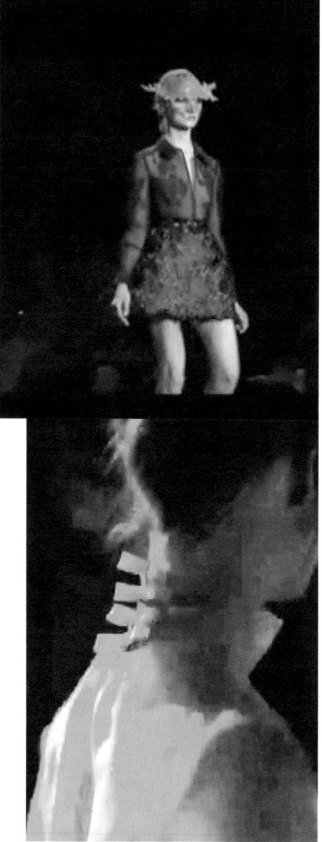

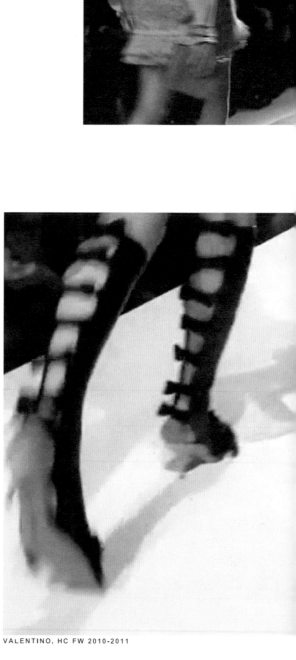

VALENTINO, HC FW 2010-2011

VALENTINO, HC FW 2010-2011

VALENTINO, HC SS 2010

VALENTINO, HC SS 2010

VALENTINO, HC FW 2010-2011

VALENTINO, HC FW 2010-2011

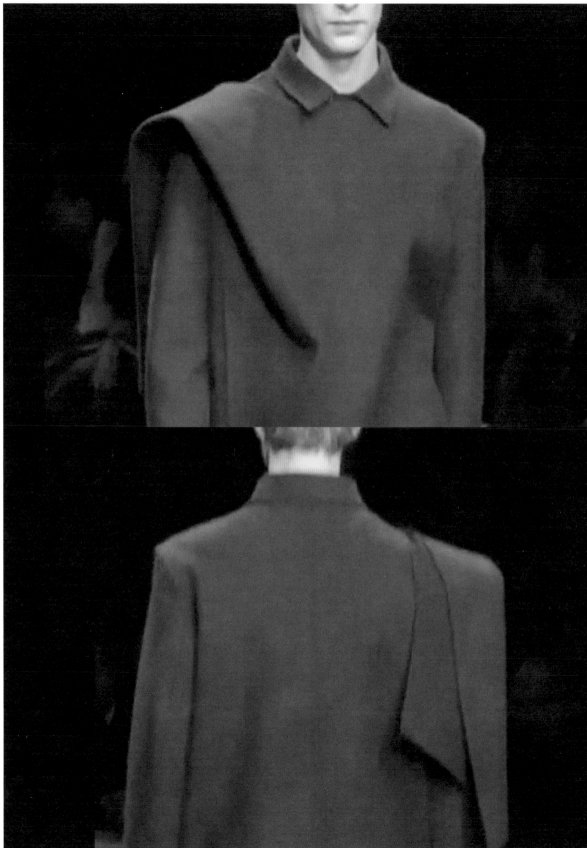

FENDI, FW 2008-2009

SS 2010

SS 2007

GIVENCHY, PAP SS 2007

74

GIVENCHY, SS 2010

GIVENCHY, SS 2010

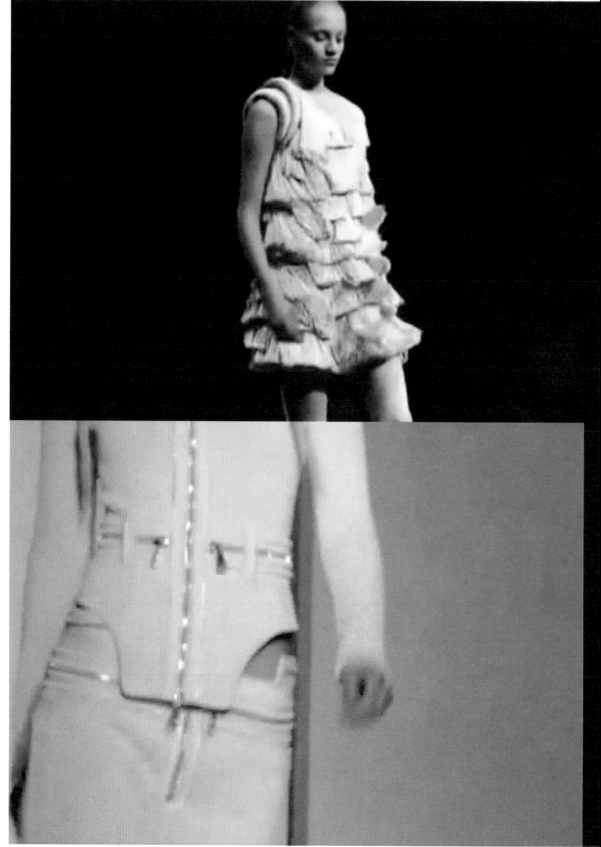

GIVENCHY, PAP SS 2011

GIVENCHY, PAP FW 2009-2010

GIVENCHY, SS 2010

GIVENCHY, HC FW 2008-2009

GIVENCHY, FW 2010-2011

GIVENCHY, PAP FW 2008-2009

GIVENCHY, PAP FW 2007-2008

GIVENCHY, SS 2011

GIVENCHY, PAP SS 2011

GIVENCHY, HC SS 2007

FERRÉ, SS 2009

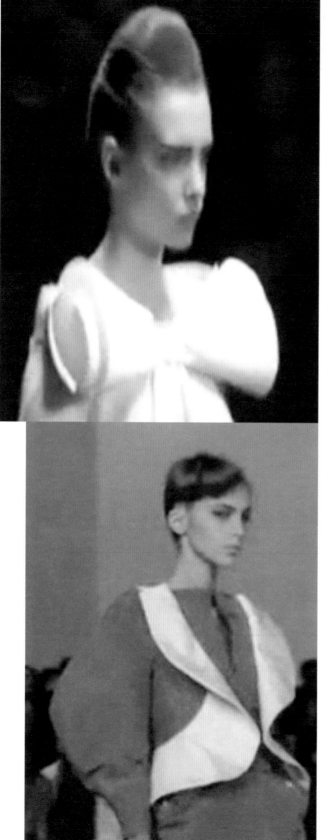

FERRÉ, SS 2009

FERRÉ, SS 2009

FW 2005-2006

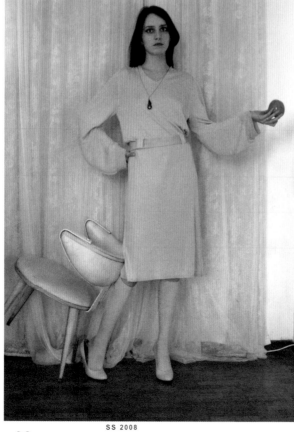

SS 2008

FW 2004-2005

HALSTON, FW 2008-2009   ROCHAS, SS 2011

Z SEGNA, SS 2010

Z SEGNA, FW 2009-2010

Z SEGNA, SS 2011

SS 20010

FW 2009-2010

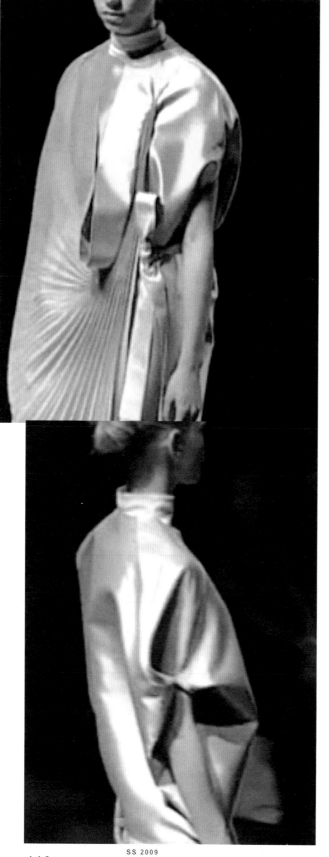

SS 2010

SS 2010

profiles: in loose order

SS 2006

SS 2007

SS 2008

FW 2006-2007

SS 2007

Albino

SS 2008

FW 2006-2007

SS 2006

FW 2007-2008

SS 2008

116

Albino D'Amato belongs to the transdisciplinary and transgenerational category of creators who, more or less consciously and critically, have decided to tackle the language of *haute couture*. The origin of the phenomenon can be traced back to the middle of the nineties, the time when the craze for vintage erupted and stylists started to influence the style of many collections through their research in the archives. As a consequence of his unorthodox training, D'Amato tackles the question of *haute couture* in a personal way. He does not reproduce the atmospheres of yesterday, as a stylist would do, and neither does he limit himself to re-creating clothes from the past *tout court*, like many of his colleagues. As an industrial designer, he concentrates instead on the definition of an object: the garment, that is, seen as a functional and self-sufficient entity in which structure, material and color interpenetrate. "Every collection springs from a different idea," he explains. "The course is not defined a priori. Sometimes I start from the form or from a material, like an architect; at others instead I take my cue from images and photographs with a strong stylistic content." The formula "contemporary *haute couture*" seems the best suited to defining Albino's work. His creations feed on the short-circuit between form and technique. While the figure alludes to nostalgic stylistic elements, the execution of the garments, carried out with the minimum of padding and cuts so that they become weightless structures, is innovative, dynamic. The result is rarefied and concrete clothing that combines the allure of the atelier with industrial mass production. In this connection d'Amato adds: "Balancing atelier and industry is a difficult task, but the result can be very interesting. Today for example certain industrial treatments look like products of the atelier. As far as commerce and creativity are concerned, on the other hand, I think they are closely correlated: what is creative can and should be commercially attractive too." Touches of the unfinished employed with restraint and experimental details that create studied imbalances characterize Albino's language. Like many of his contemporaries, the designer is constantly on the lookout for his own expressive code: in some collections the phrasing is incisive, in others delicate; it is always possible to sense a tension that is also the desire to find a precise niche in the market. (af)

Albino

Born in 1972 in Rome, he attended the faculty of Architecture. After an internship with FIAT as an industrial designer, he moved to Paris to follow the courses of the Chambre Syndicale de la Couture Parisienne. He learned the fashion craft in the ateliers of Emanuel Ungaro and Guy Laroche, and then started to work as a consultant: Giorgio Armani, Dolce & Gabbana and Versace were among his clients. In 2004, with the support of the architect Gianfranco Fenizia, he launched the Albino label. Winner of the *Who's on Next* competition in 2005, he made his debut on the catwalks of Milano Collezioni in September of the same year. From 2008 to 2010 he has been stylistic consultant of the brand Les Copains. In June 2010 he launched the Albino Deuxième collection of menswear.

6267, FW 2006-2007

6267, FW 2007-2008

6267, FW 2008-2009

6267, SS 2007

Tommaso Aquilano and Roberto Rimondi

AQUILANO.RIMONDI, PRE COLL. FW 2008-2009

6267, SS 2007

6267, SS 2008

6267, FW 2006-2007

6267, FW 2007-2008

6267, FW 2008-2009

FERRÉ, SS 2009

AQUILANO.RIMONDI, SS 2009   FERRÉ, SS 2009   FERRÉ, FW 2009-2010

AQUILANO.RIMONDI, FW 2009-2010   AQUILANO.RIMONDI, SS 2010   AQUILANO.RIMONDI, SS 2011

AQUILANO.RIMONDI, FW 2010-2011   FERRÉ, FW 2009-2010   FERRÉ, SS 2010

FERRÉ, SS 2011

FERRÉ, SS 2011

FERRÉ, FW 2010-2011

FERRÉ, FW 2010-2011

Virtuosity and technical ability are not unimportant aspects of the contemporary approach to fashion, in contrast to the tendency to make assemblage and styling crucial elements of the design. Tommaso Aquilano and Roberto Rimondi can in fact be described as "technical" designers: by training and taste, and as a result of their lengthy experience working at the heart of the system as advisors on large-scale production. Sculptural precision of line—a self-evident demonstration of skill in execution—is the salient characteristic of their work. Aquilano and Rimondi design a statuesque and imposing figure, distant in time and space; as is typical of those who have a strong style, they provoke heated and contrasting reactions. "Putting a collection together signifies understanding the changeable requirements of a diverse clientele and adapting our fund of experience," they explain. "To us it seems almost anachronistic to use the expression 'our collections'; we prefer to talk about product. We look for a tactile quality, renewing the structure not out of a forced and academic choice, but to bestow on a collection an ever different fascination that finds its expression in volume. As a consequence journeys into the modes of dress of the past assume overriding importance in the development of different solutions for construction and design." Aquilano and Rimondi's stylistic lexicon is imbued with a tension that becomes dynamic precisely because it is not resolved. On the one hand there is the avowed search for a real femininity, on the other the virtuoso self-sufficiency of the phrasing that seems to exclude, or ignore, the real world. The concentration on the product and the taste for the obsessively well-finished detail mitigate the irregularities and the abstractions, but the garments retain a cryptic allure. "At every show we try to propose again a symbolic status of the idea, presenting a product that is wearable, but not as a result ordinary. Every detail is attended to as if it were still a customized "made to measure" garment, enriched by design and consistent with wearability. It amounts to saying: creativity, construction, comfort." A conscious vein of anachronism reshuffles the cards, inviting or perhaps obliging the public to interpret things in new ways, to make unexpected and salutary changes in direction.(af)

Tommaso Aquilano and Roberto Rimondi

Born at San Severo (Aquilano) and Bologna (Rimondi), they studied at the Accademia di Costume e Moda in Rome and the Istituto Secoli in Milan respectively. They decided to work together after meeting at the Max Mara design office in 1998. They created the brand 6267, with which they won the Who's On Next competition in 2005. From 2006 to 2008 they were creative directors of Malo. In 2008, appointed creative directors of *prêt-à-porter* and women's accessories at Gianfranco Ferré, they brought the 6267 venture to a close in order to create the Aquilano.Rimondi line which, like the Gianfranco Ferré collection, they presented on the catwalks of Milano Collezioni. Since January 2009 they have been creative directors of all the Ferré lines, including menswear.

FW 2003-2004

FW 2005-2006

SS 2002

SS 2004

Boboutic

SS 06

FW 2002-2003

FW 2004-2005

SS 2005

FW 2005-2006

SS 2003

SS 2009

SS 2010

FW 2009-2010

FW 2010-2011

SS 2011

"It can't be said that we started out with the idea of knitwear. We came to knitwear by accident, and out of that accident a passion was born." This is how Michel Bergamo and Cristina Zamagni explain their choice of field. Knitwear: the most malleable of tools, capable of creating textures and forms, surfaces and lines, directly from the yarn or the fiber, in an organic process in which material and structure interpenetrate without a break, rather like what happens in architecture, the field from which they both come. Right from their first project–twenty swimsuits decorated with large ants and flies lightly embroidered with a Singer sewing machine–certain distinctive features were evident: the effort to make the object three-dimensional; the exploration of the compatibility of different materials; the taste for abstraction translated into a sort of magical realism; expressive cohesion; the choice of a clean, anti-romantic repertoire. "For us each collection is a story told in images," they explain. "We are inspired by the everyday in its simplest forms, descriptive geometry, differences, contrasts." While intensely cerebral, Boboutic's approach is not abstruse or off-putting: closer to industrial than to fashion design, the pair combine the quest for unexpected forms and volumes with the need, inescapable however inconvenient, for functionality. Angles, lines and surfaces are the bases of their stylistic alphabet; textures and colors take the place of decoration and embellishment. "Our style is: resistant, because we have been producing and distributing independently for twenty collections; refined, for the quality of the materials and the distinctiveness of the forms and volumes; ruinous, because we tear every collection to pieces mentally in order to do better with the next. All the production is carried out in small workshops that still have their basis in handicraft and that allow us to work industrially in the same manner as with hand-operated machines." The union of machine and vision, mass production and invention, is exactly what gives the Boboutic product a unique quality, one that is light but tangible. (af)

Boboutic

Both were born in 1966, Bergamo in Lugano and Zamagni in Rimini. Bergamo studied at the l'Accademia Italiana Arte, Moda e Design, but soon left; Zamagni took a diploma in photography at the Fondazione Marangoni in Florence and then went on to take a degree in architecture in the same city. They met in Florence in the early nineties. Bergamo gained a wide range of experience working as a fashion designer, while Zamagni collaborated with several art galleries and theaters. In 1999 they launched the "Wanda e Roger" project, with a production made up of one-off pieces. Out of this experience, in 2000, came the Boboutic wardrobe of knitwear. Since 2001 they have presented their creations at showrooms in Paris. They live and work in Florence. They teach in the degree course in Fashion design, Venice, Iuav University.

SS 2009

Gianluca Capannolo

SS 2010

SS 2009

SS 2010

SS 2009

SS 2009

FW 2009-2010

FW 2009-2010

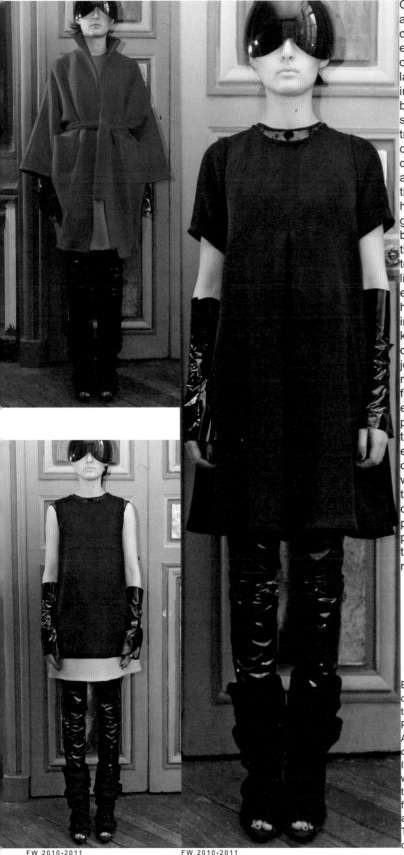

Gianluca Capannolo works, by conscious choice, in a dimension halfway between industry and handicraft. Synonymous with flexibility, the industrial atelier allows him absolute control over every phase of design. "The atelier should by definition be a laboratory of research and experimentation producing prototypes for industry," he explains. "Creativity becomes commerce when it is distributed through stores capable of understanding its essence and transmitting it to the street." He designs close-knit collections: graceful, never affected, made up of clothes of masterly quality. The forms, sometimes architectonic and clean-cut, at others fluid, revive time-honored topoi from the more or less recent history of fashion—flowing lines from the thirties and geometrical forms from the sixties are leitmotivs—but the final effect is clean, elegantly graphic rather than reliant on references to the past, and thus contemporary. Not without a hint of irony, Capannolo likes to insert eccentric variables, in a continual and elegantly controlled play of interchanges between high and low, couture and kitsch: a contrasting lining of aertex—the cellular fabric used in basketball kit—inside the bon ton coat; a sturdy industrial zipper on the double-face petite robe; precious lacquered jersey, closely resembling plastic, as material for a romantic blouse with a bow. Modularity and multi-functionality are central concepts: the different pieces of each collection, always with a clean, sharp profile, can be combined with one another, inviting the customer to compose an image quite different from the one proposed by the designer; some clothes, on the other hand, can be worn in different ways, inviting people to be creative in their use of them. Capannolo defines his style as "graphic neo-couture." He favors violent, primary colors, juxtaposed in such a way as to underline the assertive purity of the silhouette. He sums up his aesthetic in these words: "Jeans are classic, the modern petite robe!" (af)

Born in L'Aquila in 1972, he studied at the all'Accademia d'Alta Moda e d'Arte del Costume Koefia in Rome. Moving to Milan, he worked for Lambros Milona and Maurizio Pecoraro. In 2001, after a visit to Peru, he organized the Amano project, a fusion of Peruvian craft tradition and Italian design that lasted until 2003, attracting a select clientele of Italian and foreign boutiques. In 2004, relying on his contacts with a sound network of retailers, he made his debut with the collection of Gianluca Capannolo prêt-à-porter. The following year he was appointed creative director at Lancetti and in 2006 at Krizia, where he remained for three seasons. The same year he was a finalist in the *Who's On Next* competition.

VALENTINO, HC FW 2009-2010

VALENTINO, HC FW 2009-2010

VALENTINO, PAP SS 2010

VALENTINO, HC FW 2009-2010

VALENTINO, HC FW 2009-2010

Maria Grazia Chiuri
and Pier Paolo Piccioli

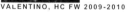

VALENTINO, HC FW 2009-2010

VALENTINO, PAP SS 2010

VALENTINO, HC FW 2(

VALENTINO, PAP SS 2010

VALENTINO, PAP SS 2010

Chiuri and Piccioli came to *prêt-à-porter* after spending a long time designing shoes and bags. The approach to the design of accessories is very different from that of clothing: there the need, in fact, is to create immediately recognizable and desirable products, sometimes resorting to the most unrestrained eclecticism. This said, the pair are not inclined toward branding pure and simple, but set out to achieve an immaterial quality: an incisive contemporariness. They aspire, in short, to turn Valentino into a cool brand. "Signor Garavani's legacy is not a simple one," they admit. "Having worked alongside him for a long time, however, we feel sufficiently in the picture with the house's language to take it in new directions." Translated into stylistic practice, the search for fresh ways, for an updated rhythm, is expressed in an abandonment of Garavani's *jolie madame* spirit in favor of trim lines, often emphasized by an unexpected, urban palette. The lightness and grace are still there, for Valentino remains the house of loose and flowing garments; but they are gently distorted. Couture pieces conceived as T-shirts, exposed zippers and mixtures of delicate and aggressive materials are some of the solutions adopted by the pair to modernize the repertoire. The crucial concept is "fusion." "We are trying to open up to unusual collaborations that allow different worlds to meet, mix and interact in harmonious dialogue," they explain. "Our vision, out of which the creative process is born, has as its protagonist a refined feminine figure, but one that is fraught with mystery. The ideas for each collection–brought together, shared and studied–are hybridized and translated not just into clothes, but into a complete expression that involves music, location, makeup and atmosphere, right up to the definition of the show." Though laudable in its intentions, the need for cross-fertilization between visual languages has not yet been turned into a true operation of design, into a stylistic synthesis, remaining limited to "styling," and thus on a purely superficial level. Moreover, an operation of this kind takes a long time and requires a complex process of trial and error in order to arrive at a new equilibrium. The impasse is to some extent clarified by their declaration of intentions: "We like the idea of the timeless: the unity of style beyond time. 'Modern' is a concept linked to an attitude, today more than ever before." (af)

Maria Grazia Chiuri
and Pier Paolo Piccioli

Born in Rome in 1964 (Chiuri) and 1967 (Piccioli), they both studied at the Istituto Europeo di Design. They met at the Fendi design studio, where they worked on accessories until 1999. It was they who were responsible for the invention of the Baguette bag. Moving to the Maison Valentino, they kept the same position, taking on in 2007, with the retirement of the couturier, the role of creative directors of all the Valentino accessory lines. In 2008 their responsibility was extended to *prêt-à-porter* and *haute couture*. Since January 2009 they have shown in Paris.

FW 2008-2009

SS 2009

Gabriele Colangelo

FW 2009-2010

FW 2008-2009

FW 2008-2009

SS 2009

FW 2009-2010

Far from the tendency to turn everything into theatrical communication, to adopt a strong expressive tone with an immediate impact, Gabriele Colangelo prefers the whisper to the shout, subtle work on the object to the sensational assemblage of "styling." His is an aesthetics of half-tones, both conceptual and chromatic, that favors slowness and introspection, and for this reason swims against the tide. "Mine is a stylistic language of hints," explains the designer, whose preference for impalpability does not exclude a marked taste for decoration, clearly expressed in his brief season with Amuleti J. "The elements that I bring into play may not be immediately perceptible, but are revealed each time in the details of the garments. The sources of inspiration for my work are of different kinds, artistic and personal. What in general attracts my curiosity and stirs my desire to experiment is craftsmanship—perhaps because of my family background—understood as an intervention of manipulation and transformation of the fabric." His family were in the fur trade, and Gabriele Colangelo's creations start out from the material: he molds it, tortures it, almost alters its DNA until he obtains surfaces with a biological, shifting, pulsating vitality. The line of the clothes, conversely, is pure: distilled to the point of sublimation of non-design, or of self-generated design, that conceals behind the effortless appearance of simplicity careful planning and a mathematically precise calculation of proportions and balances. Organic minimalism might be an apt way of defining this work. "In a certain sense creativity is ahead of the times and sometimes conveys new messages and needs. It doesn't always correspond to an immediate economic and commercial result," adds Colangelo. "Creativity represents the driving force, along with emotion, behind the dream that fashion creates, which is also the mainspring of the desire that leads people to buy. But the creative person has to have the support of the company and the industry to turn his ideas into reality: a necessary vehicle to carry the idea, producing a balance between experimental research and its application and transmission." Delicate and distant, Gabriele Colangelo's language is at once light and direct, experimental and concrete, inclusive and elusive. (af)

Gabriele Colangelo

Born in Milan in 1975, he studied classics before graduating from the Italian Fashion School of the Camera Nazionale della Moda Italiana. From 1998 to 2002 he was in charge of design at Versace Jeans Donna and collaborated with Antonio Berardi on the Extè Donna collection. From 2004 to 2008 he was creative director at Amuleti J. Winner of the *Who's on Next* competition in 2008, he has shown the Gabriele Colangelo line at Milano Collezioni since September of the same year.In February 2011 he is nominated creative director of Borbonese

CONTRADA, FW 2007-2008

CONTRADA, FW 2008-2009

CONTRADA, SS 2011

Carlo Contrada

CONTRADA, FW 2007-2008

CONTRADA, FW 2008-2009

CONTRADA, FW 2007-2008

CONTRADA, SS 2008

CONTRADA, SS 2011

"Classical is a white blouse. Modern is the way it is worn." Neutral but as sharp as a haiku, this observation sums up in crystalline fashion Carlo Contrada's approach to design as well as his wholly personal vision of style. Distilled and geometric in design, ever-changing and modular in interpretation, Contrada's work moves along a double track: at the origin of the process is technique, explored with a taste for virtuosity and for purity of line that often verges on abstraction, but without ever getting bogged down in the conceptual; at its conclusion is the person, "a contemporary, dynamic woman who cuts across boundaries." Contrada masters a borderline territory with a sure touch: he is a creator, but refrains from imposing an absolute diktat. This relativism, along with the capacity to interweave form, material and color in an impeccable manner, producing pieces as powerful as they are simple, makes him authentically contemporary. He explains: "The clothes should suggest spontaneous and functional combinations, transcending the schemes of the total look to follow the rhythms, attitudes and different requirements of life today. Each new collection starts from a vision of the materials, from an idea of weights and balances on the body. Fundamental for me are the constructions on the dummy, the visual sensation of how the material can come to life through the tailoring structure that infuses it. My style is versatile, spontaneous, refined; it is free, independent and moves between the sartorial touch and innovation." Carlo Contrada has produced a relatively small number of collections under his own label. In these, as well as in his numerous collaborations, some salient traits emerge nonetheless: the taste for rich, sophisticated colors; clean lines and a predilection for substantial but fluid fabrics; a rethinking of functionalism; disturbing touches. Flexible and always ready for a fruitful dialogue with the industry, Contrada concludes: "Creativity needs a reflection and a strategy. It cannot be totally pure because it is only the first step in a process of production. Every design starts out from a creative idea, that has to be filtered by reason, by structure and by organization in order to lead to real and concrete results." (af)

Born in Udine in 1978, he is self-taught. After a long period of training at various clothing manufacturers, where he was able to gain experience of every stage of the production process, from cutting to finishing, he made his debut in January 2007 at Altaroma with the collection that bears his name. In 2009, while his own line was temporarily put on ice, he worked as creative director of the environmentally conscious label Nathu. The same year he developed a capsule collection, which he presented at Altaroma, for the Annie company, which specializes in embroidery, reinterpreting the technique of Sicilian drawn-thread work in a contemporary key. In October 2010 he relaunched the Carlocontrada project, showing in Milan. He combines his activity as a fashion designer with that of teaching at the Iuav University in Venice.

SS 2003

FW 2003-2004

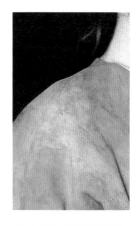

Vincenzo De Cotiis

FW 2003-2004

FW 2003-2004

FW 2004-2005

Though an architect by training, Vincenzo De Cotiis is not a designer in the rational and scientific sense of the term. Closer in feeling to an artist, or perhaps a visionary craftsman, he prefers the physical relationship with material to the abstraction of drawing. He molds pure, intensely tactile forms, following a systematic process of trial and error in which the end result is attained through incalculable progressive refinements. In this way the product retains traces of the process, in a synthesis that renders touch at least as important as sight. The aesthetic is one of reuse and recontextualization, leaning toward linearity and purism. "The materials are the starting point of each of my designs," he explains. "The research has its origin in an object from the past that I reutilize, giving it a new interpretation or using it as a base from which to create something completely new. At times the material suggests the form, at others form and material interpenetrate." In De Cotiis's work the stylistic mark is provided by the rough perfection of the finishing touches, by the unexpected associations of parts and by the use of colors that absorb the wear and tear of time. Like an industrial designer, moreover, De Cotiis concentrates on the individual piece, creating eclectic repertoires of possibilities rather than true collections with a theme, convinced that mixing styles and trends is in keeping with the contemporary image of fashion. "Rather than a style, mine is an attitude toward the construction of clothing: putting sharply contrasting materials together results in a very precise impression, sometimes dictated by the material aspect, at others by the form. I find it interesting when all this becomes recognizable." For structural reasons, De Cotiis's production occupies a position on the margins of *prêt-à-porter*, being in fact closer to the small numbers of the crafts than to the mass production of industry. "Marrying creativity and commerce is almost impossible in the big companies," he concludes. "In small-scale productions on the other hand you can still find a balance, you can draw on a know-how with a less industrial attitude." (af)

Vincenzo De Cotiis

Born in Mantua in 1958, he studied architecture at Milan Polytechnic. Right from the start he combined his work as an architect with that of fashion designer. In the early nineties he created the line Plus Jamais Ça, which in 1998 became *Haute couture*, a total look in limited editions for man and woman. In 2008 the entry of a new financial partner, and the consequent distortion of the project, led him to abandon the enterprise. After a brief interruption, he returned to fashion in 2010 with the Decotiis line, this time aimed exclusively at a female clientele. He continues to be active as both an architect and a fashion designer, mixing works done to commission with pure experimentation.

145

SS 2010

SS 2010

Marco De Vincenzo

SS 2010

SS 2010

So far Marco De Vincenzo has produced only three collections under his own name, one quite different from the other. He has done it under not the easiest of conditions, if we consider that total independence brings obstacles that are often impossible to overcome, with effects on creative output. Then his stylistic development is still in that phase of trial and error which is characteristic of the search for a personal signature. Yet some elements of his lexicon are already clear. What stands out in particular is the electric tension between simplicity and complication, between the exigencies of line and taste for decoration, this last tackled in a clean, geometric manner. The choice of materials turns on incongruous combinations—stretch lamé and velvet, Lycra and felt, for instance—and the imagery on the contrast between seductive glamour and sportswear. The range of colors, finally, is sophisticated and emphasizes, with sometimes strident contrasts, vibrant surfaces and architectonic cuts. The designer explains: "I would define my style as minimal-decorative. I like to take risks, to experiment with new forms of harmony between often dissonant colors and materials, following my natural attraction toward pure forms. I'm inspired by symmetry. I'm downright obsessed by the concept of geometric 'module': which is repeated, magnified or deformed, but basically always remains the same." On the subject of the creative process, he adds: "I can metabolize a book, an object or a journey even after a lot of time has passed, because creativity is a continuous and unstoppable flow. Everything that is left unexpressed in a collection comes back to my mind when I start on the next, adding itself to the new and to what I've not yet had the time or the courage to explore. I try to be coherent with my design and with the story I've decided to tell, without worrying about being understood by everyone and always seeking to maintain a certain unity in what I design. Italian industry is still full of resources and from season to season invests in research, placing extraordinary fabrics and materials at the disposal of designers. All you need to do is to be able to recognize and interpret them. Fashion can educate people's sense of aesthetics, not through diktats or impositions that are anti-liberal and not very modern, but through beauty, too often forgotten." De Vincenzo aims for a clear phrasing, in which the need to experiment is not translated into abstraction, but into visionary concreteness. (af)

Marco De Vincenzo

Born in Messina in 1978, he studied at the Istituto Europeo di Design in Rome. After graduating he joined the Fendi style office as an assistant to Silvia Venturini Fendi for the accessories line, a position that he still holds. In January 2009, in parallel, he made his debut in Paris with the Marco De Vincenzo line. Winner of the *Who's on Next* competition the same year, he has been on the schedule at Milano Collezioni since October 2009.

149

FW 2008-2009

FW 2009-2010

Roberta Furlanetto

SS 2010

FW 2008-2009

FW 2009-2010

FW 2008-2009

SS 2009

SS 2010

"Nothing is left to chance in my work," declares Roberta Furlanetto. Trained in the artistic field, but always interested in the manipulable physicality of textiles, Furlanetto expresses an attitude toward the design of clothing that is at once pragmatic and conceptual. Like a couturier, she works directly on the body, molding the material in a blend of precise spontaneity and controlled complication. Unlike a couturier–what she creates is ready-to-wear and she is well aware of it–she has accepted and met a difficult challenge: taking the techniques learned in the couture house, including the virtuosities of the handmade garment, and channeling them into a highly codified repertoire. To paraphrase Benjamin, Furlanetto adapts *haute couture* to the assembly line of mechanical reproduction. "The need to integrate atelier work and industrial production is not an obstacle," she explains. "I like to tackle problems of different kinds. This does not get in the way of my creativity, because the possibility of finding different solutions while acting within predetermined parameters is an enormous stimulus for me. Indeed submitting to certain limitations and getting around them helps me to go beyond my instinctive mode of operating." Aesthetics and technique interpenetrate in a dry, anti-romantic formula that does not exclude a certain feminine delicacy, expressed in the masterly contrast of purity and sumptuousness. The collections often have a dual spirit, with pieces of architectural clarity–the coats, for example, with which Furlanetto has conquered a solid niche on the market –alternating with clothes with a floral pattern and calculated explosions of flounces and pleats. "For me everything stems from the manipulation of the material," she concludes. "What I count on is experimenting, creating a personal language independent from both the diktats of the market and the very concept of season." Roberta Furlanetto has chosen a non-theatrical mode of expression, based on paring down, on intense work on the garment itself that takes the place of stuck-on, superfluous decoration, without dispensing with it entirely, and on the intrinsic passion for colors and for virtuosity that stems from her long experience in the ateliers of Paris. For this reason her work, indefinable and elusive, has the same oxymoronic nature as a theorem of geometry solved solely by means of intuition and emotion. (af)

Born at Asolo in 1965, she studied at the Accademia di Belle Arti di Brera in Milan. Working as a fabric designer for the textile manufacturer Ghioldi in Como, in 1992 she created for the latter, an art collector, a fabric made using a variety of techniques– gems, weaving, embroidery–which made such an impression on Christian Lacroix that he entrusted her with the creation of one-off pieces for his own collections of *haute couture*. As a freelance, from 1992 to 2005 she designed fabrics and special garments for the Parisian houses of Christian Lacroix, Nina Ricci, Christian Dior, Emanuel Ungaro and Azzedine Alaïa. In 2007 she launched the Roberta Furlanetto collection, to which she added a line of accessories in 2009. She shows at her own studio-showrooms in Milan and Paris.

MILA SCHÖN, SS 2011

Bianca Maria Gervasio

MILA SCHÖN, FW 2009-2010

MILA SCHÖN, SS 2011

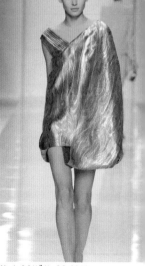

MILA SCHÖN, FW 2008-2009   MILA SCHÖN, FW 2009-2010   MILA SCHÖN, SS 2010

Bianca Maria Gervasio has spent the whole of her professional career at the Mila Schön fashion house. She has studied in depth its language, characterized by a mix of purity, experimentalism and *bon ton*, making it her own in a sort of creative symbiosis that does not exclude a personal contribution, even if restrained. Her diligent orthodoxy and preference for continuity over rupture are ideally suited to the need to design for a woman less distant than the model of the house, but consistent with its history: a contemporary figure, of a frosty and brisk elegance. "A Mila Schön collection stems from more than one factor," explains the designer. "The first is linked to the brand's history and in particular the use of double-face fabric and materials worked directly on the dummy, in three dimensions: it is the concept of the tailor-made dress. The second factor is instead the inspiration linked with concepts that are different on each occasion and shape the overall image of the collection. The intention, always, is to make the clothes lasting in time, above and beyond the tendencies and styles of the moment." Geometry is a recurrent leitmotiv: a theme, rather than a real concept, developed and interpreted on different fronts, without deviations of any kind. Sartorial constructions, prints and accessories all answer to the same inspiration, be it, for example, the kaleidoscope, or Escher's stairs. If each collection, as a complete *opus*, displays a meticulousness and a coherence that are even excessive with respect to the given theme, the individual pieces, seen as self-sufficient objects, speak a different and more rarefied language, made up of complicated simplicity and expert handling of color. The objective is to combine research and classicism, expressive urgency and attention to the particular market niche in which the brand is positioned. "Uniting creativity and commerce, industry and handicraft is never easy," declares Gervasio. "Couture for me is the idea of the blank sheet on which to design volumes and forms that industrial technicians will then turn into something easy to wear. What makes fashion of a certain level, and in particular Italian fashion, special is precisely the fact that the clothes are wearable. This factor, today, still makes the difference." Gervasio defines her own style as conceptual-volumetric. (af)

Born in Molfetta in 1979, she studied at the Istituto Marangoni in Milan. Winner of a competition for young fashion designers from Puglia in July 2003, she shows regularly at AltaRoma with the Bianca Gervasio collection. From 2004 to 2007 she was a consultant at the Mila Schön design office, where she was responsible for the lines intended for the Japanese market. At the end of 2007 she was put in charge of the Mila Schön Couture line. In this new role, she made her debut on the catwalks of Milano Collezioni in February 2008.

GUCCI, SS 2006

GUCCI, SS 2007

GUCCI, SS 2008

GUCCI, FW 2006-2007

GUCCI, SS 2007

Frida Giannini

GUCCI, SS 2008

GUCCI, FW 2007-2008

GUCCI, SS 2007

GUCCI, SS 2008

GUCCI, SS 2008

GUCCI, SS 2010

GUCCI, SS 2010

GUCCI, FW 2010-2011

Design is just one part of Frida Giannini's work within the Gucci empire. "Being able to devote my attention to several different things is stimulating," she explains. "I control everything personally, but I've also had to get used to delegating. I like to work on the collections as well as on the campaigns, on new media as well as on special projects. No choice is ever made by chance or to pursue the chimera of the cool: the necessity, always, is to keep up with the times." Far from being a position of pure convenience, but vague in character, the term "creative director" signifies for Frida Giannini a particular approach to design that naturally reflects on the quality of the work. In other words, Giannini, whose experience as a designer of accessories has inevitably shaped her way of thinking, has one prime stylistic and creative objective: inventing objects, whether clothes or accessories, that are immediately recognizable as part of the Gucci system and desirable for this reason. If at times the design is minimal, and not at all daring, it is the details that always allude to the codified iconography of the brand, bringing everything back within an unmistakable phrasing. "At every moment of my work I'm aware I'm creating something that has to be used and not end up in a museum: I think that the success with the public shows that my approach is the right one. I pay a lot of attention to what the marketing men tell me, but this doesn't mean renouncing feeling or intuition. A fashion designer should be in able to anticipate desires and speak to his or her own following." Frida Giannini owes her success—manifest and confirmed indirectly by the continual plunder to which Gucci collections are subjected by the giants of fast fashion—to a vision of luxury that could be defined as "democratic elitism": the products, consistent and with a precise design, are expensive and exclusive, but the aesthetic is never incomprehensible; on the contrary, it has a sexy and assertive look that is wholly Italian and cements its allure. "I like everything that is graphic and sharp-edged," she concludes. "The Gucci brand has a warm and Italian spirit, rooted in craftsmanship, attention to detail and quality. I try to unite this tradition with modernity." (af)

Frida Giannini

Born in Rome in 1972, she studied at the Accademia di Costume e di Moda. In 1997 she joined Fendi, where she was initially designer of the woman's wear line and then was put in charge of the leather goods one. In 2002 she moved to Gucci, as stylistic director of the handbag sector, a position that in 2004 was extended to the job description, created specially for her, of creative director of all the accessories. She was appointed creative director of women's wear in 2005, while retaining her previous role. In 2006 menswear was added to her responsibilities: thus she became sole creative director of the brand. She got the design office transferred to Rome, where she lives and works. She presents the Gucci collections in Milan.

FERRAGAMO, FW 2006-2007

FERRAGAMO, FW 2007-2008

FERRAGAMO, SS 2009

FERRAGAMO, FW 2006-2007

FERRAGAMO, SS 2008

Massimiliano Giornetti

FERRAGAMO, SS 2011

FERRAGAMO, SS 2007

FERRAGAMO, PE 2008

FERRAGAMO, SS 2007

FERRAGAMO, FW 2007-2008

FERRAGAMO, FW 2009-2010

The equation of creator and product is not always an accurate one, but in the case of Massimiliano Giornetti discretion and understatement seem to be prominent characteristics of the man's personality as well as the style of his designs. Discretion, pragmatism and calm are also the motifs of the happy encounter with Salvatore Ferragamo, the company at which Giornetti has spent almost the whole of his career. "I think that true modernity lies in being able to go back to the classical and adapt it to our own personality, needs, taste and life style," he explains. Long in charge of the men's collection alone, Giornetti has perfected a cautious but incisive phrasing, adapting the limitations that are typical of the genre–to which are added the limitations of the brand and the public it targets–to the definition of a personal mark. Lightening and cleaning the lines, focusing on impeccable accessories and a gentle process of reform, Giornetti has updated the repertory while showing unwavering respect for the tradition. "I try to create collections for a mindful customer who does not submit passively to fashion, but adjusts it to suit his own requirements and appearance: someone capable of selecting beauty and quality all by himself. Fashion is play, a luxury to be enjoyed. My goal is to create something sophisticated, elegant and intimate, but totally nonchalant. When I start on a new collection, I always try to outline a profile of the consumer to whom it is aimed: who he is, what he does, what are his passions and his interests. Keeping this profile constantly in mind, I work out the color chart and the theme so that they fit together perfectly and shape the world we have in mind." The Ferragamo archives, a rich heritage of ideas, solutions and processes, is the indispensable starting point for Giornetti's work, but he does non appear to be crushed by the weight of history. "Salvatore Ferragamo has a prestigious tradition and is known throughout the world for the superb quality and high craftsmanship of its products, united with a creativity and an innovation that are purely Italian," he concludes. "These are factors that are part of the company's DNA and cannot be ignored in my work." Giornetti applies the same type of elegant discretion, of cautious reform, to the women's collection, a course on which, however, he has only just embarked. (af)

Born in Carrara in 1971, he studied foreign languages and literature at Florence University and then fashion design at the Polimoda in the same city. After graduating he moved to Rome. He worked as an assistant to Anton Giulio Grande, looking after the high fashion and ready-to-wear collections, and then as fashion designer for a knitwear company. Returning to Florence, he went to work in the men's division of Salvatore Ferragamo, of which he became creative director in 2004. In January 2010 his responsibilities were extended to the women's division. With the fall/winter collection of 2011 he has become creative director of all the Ferragamo product lines. He shows in Milan.

FW 2005-2006

SS 2008

FW 2005-2006

SS 2008

Sara Lanzi

SS 2009

FW 2006-2007

SS 2008

FW 2006-2007

FW 2006-2007

Sara Lanzi is a woman who creates for women. The observation is not one of secondary importance: the direct experience of her own physicality, in fact, brings into play the concrete knowledge of her own body during the design process, as opposed to the idealized fantasy typical of male designers. Sara is tall and raw-boned. Her dramatic figure calls to mind medieval wooden sculpture and Alberto Giacometti. The same lean drama, absence of frills and rough delicacy can be found in the clothes she creates. "I have to admit that when I'm designing I think about what I would like to wear myself," she explains. "I'm a bit self-referential, but luckily free will then distorts everything." Sara Lanzi likes strong things, with clean lines; she pays great attention to proportions, to the balance of the silhouette. The materials she favors are few, always with a certain character, a certain solidity; the colors too are limited, solid and sober, with lively contrasts. She subtracts. She is a purist, but without extremist orthodoxies: for her the structure, the texture of the cloth take the place of the superfluous addition of decoration and ornament. "My style is at once masculine and feminine, in general fairly legible and with a strong graphic matrix. I seek balance, a harmonious state that will possess a force of its own but that, in due course, will become docile and let itself be interpreted. My collections are born out of a gradual approach. It is a subtle process of balancing and taking away. Sometimes it's an obstacle course, a compromise between visions and circumstances. it is, in any case, always a journey. I wouldn't call myself a minimalist. At least not completely. I like rigor and severity, but I don't disdain a certain delicacy. The more I grow, the more I leave my rigidity behind. Indeed I think that evolution consists in recognizing and accepting the thousand shades of gray that lie between black and white, finding your movable center that orbits with you. Sobriety, in this senses, is more a question of personality than of artistic creed." Another not negligible factor is her decision to make her base in Perugia, faraway from the nerve centers of the fashion world, and the choice of a stubborn independence that also means the adoption of a slow, personal rhythm. "From the outset I've chosen to move at my own pace, giving myself the time I need to understand the mechanisms of a fascinating but complex system. My activity is for good or ill an exact reflection of myself and this is my strength and my weakness." (af)

Born in La Spezia in 1970, she studied the conservation of the cultural heritage, taking a degree in the history of contemporary art with a thesis on Piero Gilardi. Moving to Perugia, she worked for Carpe Diem from 1999 to 2004. In 2004 she launched a line under her own name, which she presented in Paris. Winner of the *Who's on Next* competition in 2007, she is an occasional guest on the catwalks of Milano Collezioni, Milano Unica and AltaRoma. She continues to present her designs at showrooms in Paris.

2007

Leitmotiv

FW 2008-2009

2007

FW 2008-2009

2007

FW 2008-2009

2007

FW 2008-2009

SS 2009

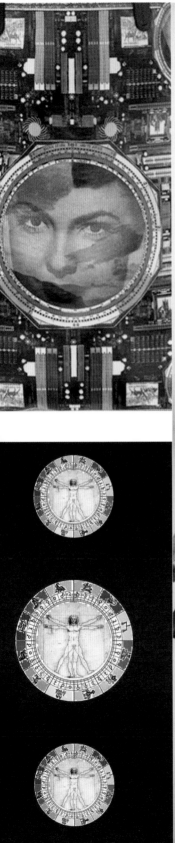

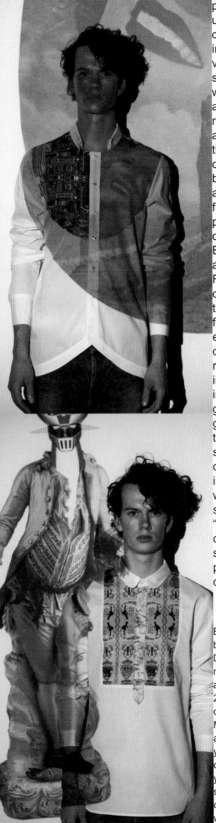

The work of Juan Caro and Fabio Sasso has a psychedelic tone that does not exclude an essential, underlying pragmatism. The combination of controlled design and dreamy decoration translates into an oblique and visionary formula. The eminently visual effect of distortion is produced by patterns that swarm all over simple pieces, twisting the surface without altering the clarity of the design. Accessories and jewelry, fundamental elements of the Leitmotiv recipe, add a further layer of visual richness. "We are inspired by people and the way they represent themselves," they say. "Our collections are born out all that surrounds us and the continual dialogue between us. These different and parallel dimensions are then transfigured by a vision that takes its cue from the history of art." All-round champions of the print, the partners of Leitmotiv fit into that peculiar channel of fashion made in Italy that starts out with Emilio Pucci and Roberta di Camerino and stretches as far as Ken Scott and the early Franco Moschino. For them prints are not a decorative ruse but a conceptual and narrative device: on each occasion they express a precise theme–the Wunderkammer, for instance, or the readymade–around which the entire collection is then constructed, even in terms of design. Lovers of the Gothic and the baroque respectively, Caro and Sasso favor two-dimensional images with a vintage flavor that they assemble into digital collages, defining a hypertrophied and glowing iconography, halfway between flamboyant goth and Victorian. Far from being dark, however, their touch is always joyful and optimistic. "Our style springs from the encounter between two different cultures and personalities, which finds expression in a cultured and eclectic language," they conclude, well aware that all this research would have no sense if it did not go beyond the drawing board. "Balancing atelier and industry, commerce and creation is essential. We pull it off by mixing limited series and easily reproducible products, always paying attention to reconciling the aesthetic and qualitative factor with salability." (af)

Born in Bogotá in 1978, Caro studied art in Colombia. Sasso, born in Busto Arsizio near Milan in 1980, graduated from the DAMS in Bologna, while learning the craft from a tailor. They met in 2002 in Bologna, where Caro was staging exhibitions and Sasso working for ateliers and theatrical companies. In 2007 they created together an installation of boxes and bags decorated with prints that they showed in Bologna and then Milan: out of this came the Leitmotiv brand of clothes and accessories, whose first collection was presented the same year. In 2008 they won the *Fashion Incubator* competition of the Camera Nazionale della Moda Italiana; the following year they were finalists in both the men's and women's wear sections of the *Who's on Next* competition and created a capsule collection for the Furla Talent Hub. In June 2010 they were finalists at the El Botón-MANGO Fashion Awards. They present their collections in Milan and Florence.

DAINESE, 2007

VIRUSLAB, SS 2011

Renato Montagner

DAINESE, 2008

VIRUSLAB, 2010

VIRUSLAB, SS 2011

VIRUSLAB, SS 2011

DAINESE, 2007

VIRUSLAB, PE 2011

DAINESE, 2007

Renato Montagner is an atypical consultant: he works in a viral way, infecting the brands with which he comes into contact, transferring spores and know-how between areas that are often distant. "With industry I earn enough to allow me to invest in the atelier and keep alive the creativity that industry expects from me," he declares. By training and approach–he is interested in the technique and methods that produce aesthetics–he is not a fashion designer in the traditional sense of the term; given the type of projects on which he works, however, he is not a pure industrial designer or architect either. Whatever the field, Montagner prefers the culture of doing: he modifies the tools, in the conviction that the only change possible is one that starts out from the way of making things. For example, the attempt, begun with Italia Independent and perfected with VirusLab, to integrate the technology of extreme sportswear with the Italian tailoring tradition has required the simultaneous adaptation of machines and techniques that has led, after a long process, to the registration of a trademark: TechnoTailormade. "The hybridizations are not just of materials, but also cultural. They are vital energy: the only way to give rise to new concepts capable of surviving crises," he explains. "Just as the virus resists antibodies because it is able to mutate and adapt, designs that incorporate new cells coming from external sectors last longer on the market." Out of necessity Montagner works in a group, often using the workshop format and integrating the know-how of different people. The ego of the designer-prophet is replaced by the chorus, while the approach is so fluid that the design of a jacket or a bicycle is developed in exactly the same way. Thus the question of style, curse of the "fashion designer," becomes secondary or consequential. "I don't believe in style for what is my field of application," he concludes. "As a consultant I have to appreciate what has been done by the firm that has called me in. I have to give it new life, not legitimate my creativity through the designs. The style is always that of the company: like a virus, I make it evolve into up-to-date forms that are coherent with the times." (af)

Born in Venice in 1963, he studied architecture at the Iuav. In 1994 he moved to Venice, California, where he and Marc Sadler founded the Venice Bleach design studio; he collaborated with Dainese and Fabbian Lighting. Returning to Italy, in 2000 he opened Changedesign, a multidisciplinary studio with branches in Venice and Milan that works in areas ranging from fashion to furnishing. Since 2003 he has been design consultant for Valextra and since 2005 art director of Dainese. In September 2007 he took part in the launch of Italia Independent in the role of art director. In 2009, appointed creative director of Pirelli PZero, he set up the experimental side project VirusLab. He teaches design for fashion and advertising at Milan Polytechnic. He teaches in the degree course in Fashion design, Iuav University.

VIONNET, SS 2011

VIONNET, FW 2010-2011

Rodolfo Paglialunga

VIONNET, FW 2010-2011

VIONNET, SS 2011

VIONNET, FW 2010-2011   VIONNET, SS 2010   VIONNET, FW 2010- 2011

The case of Rodolfo Paglialunga is similar to that of many designers now in their thirties and forties who have made their way through the ranks and finally come into the limelight, but have never been tempted to make a go of it on their own. In fact the role of creative director, however much freedom is granted, entails a different sort of involvement than that of total independence, simply because the need to express your own vision is constrained within a preexisting framework; an elastic one certainly, but one that cannot be ignored. While conscious of the limitations, Rodolfo Paglialunga does not seem bothered by them. "As a designer I've never really though about doing a line in my own name," he explains. "In the Maison Vionnet I feel protected and the historic nature of the brand offers me very great exposure. Which does not mean, of course, that the commitment is any less. On the contrary, it's double." In fact the designer has to deal with a complex legacy: that of a legendary fashion house which remained silent for several decades and then was artificially resuscitated after a long period of hibernation. "Vionnet is a name to conjure with, but also a house that has been preserved by spurious interpretations barring a double false start, with Sophia Kokosalaki and Marc Audibet, *editor's note*]. Taking on a brand with such a history required a fair amount of daring. I made a thorough study of Madeleine Vionnet's work, of her approach to the cut and her way of getting clothing and body to hold a dialogue. At a certain point, however, I sort of forgot it, in order to avoid too faithful and literal an interpretation. I try to pick out the essential elements of Vionnet's work: lightness and femininity in the first place. The color on the other hand is my personal addition." Paglialunga is fond of complicated simplicity and unexpected but always graceful and elegant combinations of colors; he favors clean lines and a purity that is never established a priori but the fruit of a long process of editing, of never-ending work carried out directly on the dummy, fusing concept and manual skill in a praxis of doing things in 3D. The processual character of this approach is in a way the distinctive mark of this designer, who strews finished garments with controlled touches of the unfinished, avoiding the rigidities of *haute couture* while he rereads and reveals the secrets of work in the atelier. "Indefiniteness is often the character that makes a garment special, that gives it soul," he concludes. "In fashion the industry could not exist without the work of the atelier. Creativity is my mode of being, the market the means that allows me to reach as many women as possible." (af)

Born in Tolentino in 1967, he studied at the Istituto Marangoni in Milan. From 1993 to 1995 he was an assistant to Romeo Gigli. In 1996 he joined Prada, where he remained until 2008, in the position of creative director of the women's wear collection. In February 2009 he was appointed creative director of Vionnet, the French fashion house relaunched by an Italian management headed by Matteo Marzotto and Gianni Castiglioni. Since October 2009 he has presented the Vionnet collection in Paris.

YSL, SS 2005

YSL, FW 2006-2007

YSL, SS 2006

YSL, FW 2005-2006

Stefano Pilati

YSL, FW 2007-2008

YSL, SS 2006

YSL, FW 2005-2006

YSL, SS 2007

YSL, SS 2005

YSL, FW 2006-2007

YSL, SS 2007

YSL, SS 2009

YSL, FW 2009-2010

YSL, SS 2010

YSL, FW 2009-2010

YSL, FW 2009-2010

YSL, SS 2010

YSL, SS 2010

YSL, FW 2010-2011

YSL, FW 2010-2011

YSL, SS 2011

YSL, SS 2011

The symbolic but unsettling tension of the encounter with paternal, domineering figures is something that runs through the whole of Stefano Pilati's career, charging his creations with an energy stemming from the continual friction between the quest for a classical phrasing and its ostentatious negation, between orthodoxy and the need for independence.

In this sense his appointment as head of the Maison Saint-Laurent has represented the most difficult challenge of all, for the man as well as the designer, finding expression in a natural or deliberate osmosis with Monsieur Saint-Laurent. The tormented inwardness, the obsession with the rigor of masculine chic contradicted by surrenders to a flowery voluptuousness and love of elegance are just some of the points of contact between the two. Speaking of what inspires him, Pilati explains: "Everything. In particular, the sense of inferiority I feel toward culture, knowledge. The imagery of daily life, the result of contortionist poses of self-celebration and the pursuit of success, prompt me to develop my work in an ever more objective, abstract and detached direction." Abstraction and detachment are terms that define his work well: the lines are clean, the volumes sculptural; substantial, dull, masculine fabrics or the exact opposite; the whole associated with an austere decorative reserve. If in the women's wear collections the relationship with the YSL archives is filtered to the point of absolute rarefaction, in the men's ones it is consciously obliterated: using himself as a model, Pilati defines instead the figure of a contemporary dandy who defends himself behind the haughty armor of extreme elegance. "A collection," he declares, "stems from the elaboration of a creative process aimed at holding a dialogue with consumers. Images, ideas, instincts, experiences and method are expressed, maintaining a balance between past and present, history and contemporaneity, classicism and modernity." Inclined to striking a pose, Pilati nevertheless makes good use of the training he received in the trenches of manufacturing: "in the textile industry there is a widespread dedication that is a true national treasure." And he concludes: "The textile industry suffers from the effects of globalization in monastic silence, but does not forgo the challenge. I would not be where I am if it were not for the Italian manufacturing industry. The atelier is a universe in itself: the framework of my ideas, a reality without which the biomechanical qualities of the fashion vehicle would not exist." (af)

Stefano Pilati

Born in Milan in 1965, he is self-taught. At the age of just sixteen, he was given an internship with Nino Cerruti and subsequently worked at various textile manufacturers. In 1993 he became an assistant to Giorgio Armani for the menswear collection. In 1995 Miuccia Prada hired him to supervise research into fabrics, promoting him in 1998 to the role of designer of the Miu Miu men's and women's collections. In 2000 he was called by Tom Ford to move to Paris and join the Yves Saint-Laurent team. Promoted in 2002 to the post of head of design of all the lines, in 2004, following Ford's exit, he was appointed creative director of the house. He lives and works in Paris.

FW 2006-2007

FW 2007-2008

Fabio Quaranta

FW 2007-2008

FW 2006-2007

FW 2007-2008

FW 2006-2007

SS 2007

FW 2011-2012

Discreet: this is the succinct adjective that Fabio Quaranta uses to define his own style, adding that he creates his clothes "for the common man." Common, let's be clear, only in the sense that he is not talking about an idealized and unattainable figure, the kind that too often alienates niche designers from the real public and that, in another context, is used by the rhetoric of the major brands to create the mirage of an attractive lifestyle and trigger the craving to buy. In Fabio Quaranta's work, in fact, there is no trace of the common in the sense of ordinary, and the designer is perfectly conscious of this. He explains: "I'm inspired by everyday life, relationships with people, the people themselves, a song, a movie, work, an image, a stranger." This variety of inputs, filtered by an honest and direct sensibility, translates into a refined but earthy language, poetically concrete in the choice of colors and the insistence on the tactile experience of wearing the garment. Conceptually a member of the brutalist school of menswear that unites in the name of research figures as different, even contrasting, as Carol Christian Poell, Julius and Attachment, Quaranta renounces the intransigence of his colleagues in order to adopt a conciliatory approach. "It neither surprises nor irritates me to see my clothes interpreted in a different way from the one I had imagined," he declares. "In the store its common for me to watch the systematic dismembering of a collection by the customers, but I hold that this is a great lesson for any creator." The search for a signature expressive characteristic coincides for Fabio Quaranta with the aspiration to design clothes that fuse organically with the personality, creating a feeling with the body and its movements. His is an experiment in simplification of the iconic male wardrobe—uniforms and workwear are clear references—reduced to the crudest essence in order to bring out as characterizing traits, at once structural and unexpectedly decorative, the texture of the cloth and the details of the construction. In this sense, Fabio Quaranta is a genuine minimalist. (af)

Born in Rome in 1977, he is self-taught. After graduating in business economics from Roma Tre University, he worked for two years as a menswear buyer for the Degli Effetti boutique. In 2004 he presented a prototype of the Converse All-Star covered with vinyl in Paris that proved a great success. He went on to collaborate with Maurizio Altieri of Carpe Diem on the Evoluzione project. In January 2006 he made his debut, again in Paris, with the FQR collection of men's prêt-à-porter. The same year he inaugurated the Motelsalieri multifunctional structure in Rome, in which he opened a men's clothing and accessories store in 2009 with his wife, Grace Fisher. Winner of the second Who's on Next/Menswear competition in 2010, he changed the name of his line to Fabio Quaranta. He combines his activity as a fashion designer with those of artist, performer and he teaches at the degree course in Fashion Design at the Iuav University, Venice.

MARVIELAB, 2007

MARVIELAB, 2009

Mariavittoria Sargentini

MARVIELAB, 2007

MARVIELAB, 2009

MARVIELAB, 2007

MARVIELAB, 2008

MARVIELAB, 2010

178

Brevity, concision and renunciation of the superfluous are the characteristic features of Mariavittoria Sargentini's work. The relentless mechanicalness of Agota Kristóf's prose offers an apt comparison: the emotive and emotional aspect of the creative act is deliberately erased; the design seems to be determined in a logical, automatic way from a precise series of premises. In this sense the decision to call her base of operations a "laboratory," not an atelier, is significant. Sargentini does not create true collections, but designs, often not linked to any season. Suspension–in space, in gender, in time–is a prominent trait: her layered coats that can be taken apart, for instance, are designed for use in the summer as well as the winter and are habitats at least as much as they are clothes; the trouser suits with disorderly cuts ignore the trite distinction between masculine and feminine. "The designs that come out of the Marvielab research laboratory are the result of a study of form and function," she explains. "Out of the breaking up and reassembly of classic items of clothing are born objects that are developed around the person and the everyday act of dressing. What I propose is a 'conscious dressing,' fruit of an investigation of the relationship between individual and clothing: the person as three-dimensional form, the garment as flat form; the garment as variable element, the person as modifiable form. In their mutual interaction, the body finds its own 'dressability' and the clothing its own personality. It is a visual and sensorial experimentation generated from essential constructions accompanied by natural materials, wearable in any season. The objective is to create something pure and comfortable." Sargentini defines his style as minimal and individual: minimal, because the design has a utilitarian component that shuns ephemeral vogues and fleeting frivolities; individual, because it is the customer who creates forms and volumes, in his or her use of the garment. Renunciation of the limelight and choice of a discreet tone assume the character of a moral imperative: Sargentini takes a step back, even forgoing the proposal of a precise silhouette; her message is broad and inclusive. In a way this reticence places her outside fashion, understood as an abstract system of signs, and brings her closer to the pragmatic qualities of clothing, which she sees in terms of the design of a functional object. "Real": this is the adjective that Mariavittoria uses to describe the essence of her work. (af)

Born in Perugia in 1976, she studied at the Politecnico della Moda e del Costume in Florence, going on to take an Arts degree at the university of the same city. After spending two years at Alghero as an assistant to Antonio Marras, she was back in Perugia, working for Carpe Diem. In September 2006 she set up the Marvielab design laboratory. In June 2009 she was a finalist in the *Who's on Next / Uomo* competition the first time it was held. She lives and works in Perugia. She presents her collections in Paris. She teaches degree course in Fashion design, Iuav University, Venice.

Z ZEGNA, SS 2010

Z ZEGNA, FW 2007-2008

Z ZEGNA, FW 2008-2009

Z ZEGNA, SS 2008

Z ZEGNA, SS 2011

Alessandro Sartori

Z ZEGNA, SS 2009

Z ZEGNA, SS 2011

Z ZEGNA, SS 2008

Z ZEGNA, SS 2010

Z ZEGNA, FW 2007-2008

Z ZEGNA, FW 2008-

Today's most advanced menswear, as remote from the stiffness of traditional tailoring as it is from the repugnant hysteria of the avant-garde, represents a surmounting of outdated categories and dichotomies–classical/fashionable, formal/casual–and a move toward their reconciliation. Alessandro Sartori's work can be assigned to this current. He defines his approach as "futurist tailoring." A vivid trim on the sartorial double-breasted jacket; a duplicated panel to create a pattern of mock overlays; cuts that reveal, instead of concealing, the sum of parts that make up the garment; reconsidered proportions: it is by using elements and variables of this kind that Sartori defines new balances that amount to sketching the outlines of a softer, but still solid masculinity. He explains: "I love the beauty of the classical projected into our imminent future. The classical is what all of us have seen, admired, studied and sought to understand. The modern is a style that is fresh and pleasing today, just perfect for the moment to which it refers."

The entire course of Sartori's professional and stylistic development has taken place within that temple of Italian classicism that is Ermenegildo Zegna. Sartori displays on the one hand a profound understanding of the brand's heritage, on the other a realization of the urgent need to communicate with a new following, closer to his own personality and sensibility. "Zegna stands for authenticity, reliability, quality and tradition: characteristics that the public associates with the label and that I try to respect. When I came up with the Z Zegna project the idea was to meet the needs of a new customer with a product, absent from the market at the time, of research carried out following the canons of the luxury one." The principle translates into a trim, clean line; into clothes with sober colors, as tradition demands. Understatement and lavishness are once again reconciled, instead of excluding one another. "The Italian character is a key feature," concludes Sartori, "as is a certain absence of drama. Everything turns around an idea of refined nonchalance, of elegance as play. There is still an Italian touch in fashion: I would say that it is as if the culture of our teachers and our tailors had remained foremost in our thoughts." (af)

Born in Biella in 1966, he studied in Milan. After gaining experience as a textile designer at the Lanificio Mario Zegna and an assistant fashion designer at Ermenegildo Zegna, he spent the years from 1991 to 1993 in Hong Kong, where he worked as a freelance consultant. Returning to Italy, he worked with Zegna. From 1993 to 1997 he designed the Ermenegildo Zegna and Zegna Soft lines; from 1997 to 2003 he was product and style director of Zegna Soft. In 2004 he came up with the idea of the Z Zegna project, of which he is creative director. After a few seasons at Pitti Uomo, the line made its debut on the catwalks in New York in 2007. Since June 2009 Z Zegna has been on the calendar at Milano Collezioni Uomo.

FW 2008-2009

FW 2008-2009

Francesco Scognamiglio

FW 2008-2009

SS 2009

FW 2008-2009

SS 2009

182

High, sophisticated, aimed at a niche market: that is how Francesco Scognamiglio defines his style. His language is theatrical, dramatic; his woman, a cruel and unattainable *femme fatale*. Here once again we have a designer who draws on the repertoire of *haute couture*, reinterpreted in this case from a rock-rococo angle. "I was born a couturier and that's how I feel, even though I'm perfectly well aware of working for industry," he explains. "For me modernity means bringing the classical, the past, back to life, modulating it on forms and volumes that make it contemporary. Today it's necessary to pay a great deal of attention to establishing the right balance between style and marketing of the product. The difficulty lies in creating a precise and recognizable identity that can at the same time have a positive response on the market." Statuesque glamour and carnal sensuality–in a version that is sometimes incisive and direct, at others sensational and distorted–are the immediately recognizable traits of Scognamiglio's work. The designer's steadfast aim is to win himself a place in the international category of the avant-garde neo-couturier, fulfilling a desire, not expressed but tangible, to break out of a certain Italian provincialism. The line of his clothes is clear-cut: the silhouette, voluptuous and hyper-feminine, arises from a careful study of form and volume in which the decoration is integral to the structure, not a gratuitous addition. Sleeves, collars and necklines lend themselves to sometimes daring experiments with volumes that Scognamiglio contains within a rigorous and controlled design, reshuffling the cards with dissonant touches: he mixes latex and crystals, for example, or romantic flounces and shameless exposure of the thighs. This said, it remains to be determined whether his approach is really avant-garde. The term "avant-garde" is widely misused in fashion; in Scognamiglio's case, moreover, the avant-gardism seems to be limited essentially to certain choices of styling for the show, the accessories and the use of incongruous materials: traits that have made him the darling of the stylists of international show business, in particular Arianne Phillips and Nicola Formichetti, who collaborate with Madonna and Lady Gaga respectively. But the styling is an add-on, an extra. The line of the clothes expresses a different propensity. And so the most apt definition seems to be the one given by the designer himself: "Mine is a classical elegance... in my own way." (af)

Francesco Scognamiglio

Born in Pompeii in 1975, he studied at the Istituto Superiore di Design in Naples. In 1998 he opened his own atelier of high fashion in the same city and two years later made his debut on the catwalks of AltaRoma. In March 2001 he moved on to ready-to-wear, which he presented in Milan. Right from the beginning of his career, he combined his freelance activity with that of consultant and creative director: his clients have included the Versace, Verri and Allegri brands. The relationship with Allegri continues today. An accord with a new financial partner in 2008 has guaranteed the label a sound structure that coincides with renewed exposure in the media and a strengthening of distribution.

SS 2009

SS 2011

Gianni Serra

SS 2011

SS 2009

SS 2009

FW 2010-2011

SS 2010

186

Chronologically a child of the multichannel generation, the one that grew up in the eighties of the frenzied cut-up, the ideology of betrayal and the breakdown of barriers, Gianni Serra likes contrasts, incongruous combinations and hybridizations. He designs clothes with a precise line and a taste for controlled complication that seems to be guided by purely visual requirements; he compresses the emotion of the creative impulse into a tense but composed sign that is often crude and abrasive. And yet the designer points to the female body and the idealized structure of the elements that make up the wardrobe as the keystones of his research. He explains: "I prefer not to have anything predefined when I tackle a design, but to be able to mix elements and forms to obtain new visual codes."

Contrast is at once the strength and the weakness of Serra's language. The key lies in the electric gap that exists between the physical concreteness of the body and the abstraction of the line. On the one hand, it is the purity of the clean and affirmative design that dominates. The figure is created as a sum of parts, each with a precise tactile and chromatic character, underlined by a sparing use of prints and color; some elements of the garment are emphasized, isolated, while others are contorted, obliterated. On the other hand, the careful consideration of female physicality means that his experimentalism remains anchored to an everyday, comprehensible dimension. The play of contrasts and fusions is recapitulated in the research into material. "I like to couple classical and pure materials with technical and avant-garde ones. I create classical structures with daring materials to uproot the image and give the clothing an up-to-date and unusual aspect: a man's jacket and pair of trousers in a coated fabric, for example. Or I use the most classical of men's textiles like extra-fine Tasmanian wool for balloon clothes and pleated flounces."

Still in search of an expressive synthesis—which explains the marked eclecticism of the few collections he has produced so far—Serra works in a wholly personal manner on catching people off their guard. Classical and experimental, masculine and feminine, simplification and complication, structure and deconstruction are all elements of his clean and antinostalgic repertoire. (af)

Born in Alghero in 1970, he studied at the Istituto Marangoni in Milan. In 1993 he moved to Rome to open an atelier. He worked for a private clientele, made costumes for theatrical productions, collaborated with artists and tried his hand as a stylist, accumulating a varied range of experiences. Between 1995 and 2005 he was present on the catwalks of AltaRoma with the *haute couture* collection that bore his name. In 2008, back in Milan, he launched the GIANNISERRA brand of *prêt-à-porter*, produced entirely in Italy. A finalist in the *Who's on Next* competition in 2009, at the end of the same year he won the support of the distributor Daniele Ghiselli, who is still his patron.

RICCARDO TISCI, FW 2005

GIVENCHY, PAP SS 2006

GIVENCHY, PAP SS 2008

GIVENCHY, PAP FW 2006-2007

RICCARDO TISCI, PAP FW 2005-2006

Riccardo Tisci

GIVENCHY, PAP SS 2007

RICCARDO TISCI, FW 2005-2006

GIVENCHY, PAP FW 2006-2007

RICCARDO TISCI, FW 2005

GIVENCHY, PAP FW 2009-2010

GIVENCHY, PAP SS 2008

GIVENCHY, PAP FW 2007-2008

GIVENCHY, PAP FW 2008-20(

GIVENCHY, PAP SS 2009

GIVENCHY, PAP FW 2007-2008

GIVENCHY, PAP FW 2008-2009

GIVENCHY, PAP SS 2009   GIVENCHY, PAP FW 2010-2011   GIVENCHY, HC FW 2010-2011

GIVENCHY, PAP SS 2010

GIVENCHY, PAP SS 2011

GIVENCHY, PAP SS 2010

GIVENCHY, PAP FW 2010-2011

GIVENCHY, PAP FW 2010-2011

GIVENCHY, PAP FW 2010-2011   GIVENCHY, PAP SS 2011   GIVENCHY, PAP SS 2011

The influence of the sociocultural environment on the imagery and language of a creator is not something that can be neglected. Even though he grew up in Como, for example, Riccardo Tisci considers himself, with some pride, a man of the South. The city of origin of his family, who moved to the North shortly before his birth, is Taranto, a place symbolic of that land of sorrow that is Salento, a region of touches of freedom and wild sensuality, of Dionysian abandon and Catholic bigotry. It is on this ancestral culture that Tisci draws copiously, while also borrowing—with that taste for miscegenation typical of the channel-hopping generation—from the macabre affectations of Victorian aesthetics and the metropolitan rituality of the sadomasochist. Religion, sexuality and perversion are recurrent elements of his language; the phrasing– dense and assertive in the few collections in his name–has been progressively toned down at Givenchy, but without losing its force. Tisci is interested in the physicality of the relationship between body and clothing, a physicality that can even be violent, as well as in the intrinsic one of the garment as object, heightened through the intense treatment of surfaces and decorations. "My priority is not to create something beautiful, but to allow women to express themselves physically in my clothes. Beauty, for me, comes from this language of the body." This is how Tisci defines the essence of his work, in the words of Marina Abramović during a recent event at the MoMA. Invited to describe his style, he chooses four adjectives: dark, romantic, sexual, mystical. "Contrast" is another key concept: the categories of beautiful/ugly are turned completely on their head, replaced by the quest for a predatory, statuesque and disturbing glamour, concealed behind the composure and the nonchalance required by the brand. The same pathos can be found in his menswear collections, a mix of tailoring and street wear designed for a hitherto widely neglected clientele of men who are fashion conscious but little accustomed to the formal. Not lacking a head for business, Tisci concludes: "Creativity and commerce go hand in hand. If it is frustrating for a designer to create without selling, it is equally so for a customer to buy something banal." (af)

Riccardo Tisci

Born in Como in 1974, he studied at Central Saint Martins College in London. After graduation he created one-off pieces for the Kokon to Zai boutique with the label Riccardo Tisci. Returning to Italy, he assisted Antonio Berardi and Stefano Guerriero and then became head designer at Coccapani and PUMA Rudolf Dassler Schuhfabrik. In May 2004 he was appointed creative director of Ruffo Research. The failure of the project to get off the ground prompted him to relaunch the line in his own name, which he presented in Milan in October 2004. In the spring of 2005, after just two shows with the Riccardo Tisci brand, he was appointed artistic director of Givenchy women's *prêt-à-porter* and *haute couture.* In 2008 his contract was renewed with a broader mandate that also comprised men's *prêt-à-porter* and accessories. He lives and works in Paris.

SS 2006

FW 2007-2008

FW 2010-2011

SS 2008

SS 2006

Isabella Tonchi

FW 2010-2011

SS 2006

SS 2011

SS 2006

FW 2007-2008

FW 2010-2011

On her website Isabella Tonchi portrays herself with a short video. The slogan at the beginning declares "Fashion is communication": Isabella illustrates this on a mood board–the wall covered with sources of inspiration that sums the atmosphere of a collection–in which images of pleated skirts and motorcycle jackets are mixed up with photographs of Pina Bausch and documents of the British youthquake of the sixties. What stands out most in this visual and conceptual collage is the juxtaposition, made all the more energetic by its incongruity, of extreme classicism and vitriolic rebellion. Isabella Tonchi's style, in fact, is contained in the elastic gap between worlds that never touch one another: contrast is her expressive key, but the sometimes violent friction between discordant elements is resolved in a composed and calm phrasing, electric but never shocking, classical with a twist. She explains: "My style is a blend of innocence and provocation. I'm inspired by the way people dress, what they communicate through the clothes they wear, be they folk, representative of an era or characteristic of a minority or a single individual. Each of my collections is a story that comes to life through clothing made up of proportions, fabrics and colors." The attention to the "ethnographic" aspect of the daily performance of dressing places Isabella Tonchi in an area strongly influenced by Britain, and more specifically London. The impact of the city on the underground fashion of the eighties, the milieu in which Tonchi was formed, is moreover undeniable. Yet Tonchi has succeeded in channeling her radicalism into a formula that is comprehensible and not stubbornly focused on a particular niche, but without forgetting its roots or renouncing the alternative touch. Molded by her long experience as a consultant, Tonchi handles the art of compromise deftly, showing herself capable of marrying expressive needs and market requirements. However, she prefers small numbers and evolution by tiny increments to the hysteria of coming up with something new every six months, conscious that small-scale revolutions are the ones that last. She concludes: "Creativity and commerce are dependent on one another. Creativity becomes communicable through commerce, while the atelier is the breeding ground of ideas for industry. The two aspects balance each other through a compromise between invention and producibility." (af)

Born in Florence in 1963, she is self-taught. In 1982, after finishing language school, she met Elio Fiorucci, who invited her to come to Milan, where for six years she was responsible for the design of the Fiorucci Donna collection. In 1988 she started to work as a freelance consultant and designer, developing projects and capsule collections for brands like Uniform, Malo, Sportswear International and Benetton. From 1991 to 1993 she was design director of the G Gigli line, and then of NN Studio. In 1993 she worked with Miuccia Prada on the Miu Miu project, which she followed until 1996, going on to take charge of cK and Versus. In 2003 she launched the Isabella Tonchi line, which she presents in Milan, New York and Paris.

FW 2005-2006

SS 2006

Giambattista Valli

FW 2006-2007

FW 2005-2006

FW 2005-2006

SS 2006

FW 2006-2007

Haute couture, in contemporary fashion, is often a definition of pure convenience, a high-flown formula used to cover up the rehashing of trite and anachronistic stylistic features. Giambattista Valli tackles the problem from a different perspective. Despite having modeled the mythology of his personality on the figure of the couturier—the choice to make Paris his base is, in this sense, highly significant—Valli is in fact conscious of operating within an industrial system. He explains "I'm interested in the tailoring side of the garment, and this is as true for an evening dress as it is for a T-shirt: it's a matter of approach. I was also one of the first, however, to fuse the cultural experience and religious rituality of the historic ateliers with the rapidity demanded by the contemporary market. The relationship between creativity and commerce is a crucial point: I've never been attracted by museum-style discourses on the catwalk; I prefer to go into a woman's wardrobe first." A statement as lucid as it is provocative, if you consider that Valli likes to surround himself, as a couturier, with the *crème de la crème* of society and the aristocracy. In fact contrast and contradiction are key themes in the imagination of this designer, who cites Francis Bacon, Nan Goldin, Fellini, Warhol and MTV as obsessions and inspirations, but also keeps in mind the lessons of Yves Saint-Laurent, Halston, Roberto Capucci and Emanuel Ungaro. Giambattista Valli designs persistent silhouettes that have a forceful impact on the gaze of the observer. The body is the pivot of his research; not infrequently his desire to experiment is so strong that it verges on body modification, but in a setting of elegance and grace; the surfaces are dense and vibrant, the colors assertive. "I always work on the tailor's bust, which has a series of lines running across hips, breast and waist. In each collection I try to highlight one of those lines, keeping in mind my typical silhouette, which is dual: androgynous and spindly like a pencil stroke, or blooming like a bouquet or a bunch of feathers. I would define my style as timeless: poised between past and present; ageless: it is a philosophy, a mental, not a physical stance; effortless: fluid, as style in general should be, spontaneous, free of planning, totally unconscious." Dramatic, it's worth adding. (af)

Giambattista Valli

Born in Rome, he studied at the Istituto Europeo di Design in Rome and Central Saint Martins College in London. In 1987 he was assistant to Roberto Capucci, and then for five years head designer of the Fendissime line. In 1995 he moved to Milan, where he was senior designer for Krizia. In 1997 he went to Paris, where he still lives today, to work with Emanuel Ungaro, at first under the master's wing and then, from 2001, in his own right, as creative director of the ready-to-wear collections, accessories and Ungaro Fever. In March 2005 he launched the Giambattista Valli line, which since then he has presented on the calendar in Paris.

BLACKDRAGON, FW 2010-2011   BLACKDRAGON, FW 2010-2011   GUY ROVER, FW 2010-2011

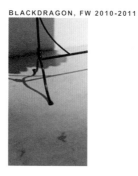  

BLACKDRAGON, FW 2010-2011

Franco Verzì

L'ESKIMO, SS 2010

BLACKDRAGON, FW 2010-2011   BLACKDRAGON, FW 2010-2011   GUY ROVER, FW 2010-2011

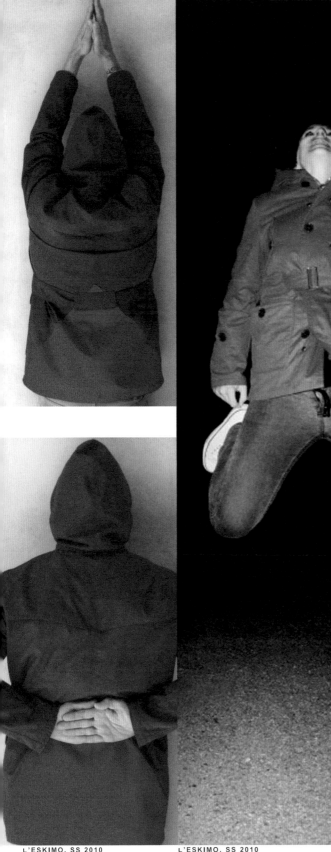

Not a simple and anonymous consultant, nor a designer with his name emblazoned on the label, Franco Verzì develops specific projects with a series of different partners: capsule collections, experiments in cobranding and rebranding and image renewal. For him the problem of style as quest for a personal code of expression assumes a meaning different from the commonly accepted notion: a more fluid and changeable one, if you like, but no less stringent as a result. He explains: "My objective, once I have analyzed thoroughly the company I am going to be working with, is to find the way to accompany the creative idea with a suitable action, creating a personal numerical code that cuts across boundaries and is specific to the project. The approach to the culture of design is decisive in contextualizing the fusion between the requirements of the client and my stylistic characteristics: I try to give freshness to simple, sometimes classical objects, bringing an innovative touch to forms or cuts. In my work you can sense, in general, a strong flavor of "sartorial deconstruction," and this affects not just the product and the graphics, but also the architecture, design and marketing." Viral and mutable, Franco Verzì's designs require a preexisting framework–that of the brand which he chooses as a partner each time–to come to life, in a dialogue in which the tension between tradition and innovation–or to put it another way between stasis and dynamism–is the indispensable mainspring of the creative process and the justification of its outcome. Verzì's work, in this sense, shows that apparently limited situations are precisely the ones that create ferment and possibility. "I choose the partner with which to collaborate after a careful examination of its corporate and strategic tradition, but above all in reference to the possibility of creatively and tactically coordinating every component of the project," he explains. "Usually, though, I respond to a call from the entrepreneur who has decided to bring his company into the market of special ideas." A dialogue that is not always easy and not always possible. For this reason Franco Verzì has carved himself out, with Equipe 70, an independent space of expression, but once again within a framework that has precise limits: the parka, and everything that turns around it. (af)

Born in Trieste in 1965, he is self-taught. After attending art school, he worked in the family stores, refining the knowledge of tailoring he had learnt from his father with direct experience of retailing. In 1992 he moved to Riccione, where he still lives and works, and set up the F03 consultancy studio, active in the fields of design and retail. SUN68, Aishti, Fluo and Valstarino are some of his most successful projects. Currently he is in charge of the *BLACKDRAGON capsule collection for Grifoni Denim and the Equipe 70/l'eskimo and D'amico Bologna projects, as well as creative director of Guy Rover.

SOFTCORE, SS 2008

SERGIO ZAMBON, FW 2010-2011

SERGIO ZAMBON, SS 2010

FENDI, FW 2008-2009

SERGIO ZAMBON, FW 2010-2011

Sergio Zambon

SERGIO ZAMBON, SS 2011

FENDI, FW 2007-2008

SERGIO ZAMBON, FW 2010-2011

SOFTCORE, FW 2008-2009

SOFTCORE, FW 2008-2009

SERGIO ZAMBON, SS 2011

Sergio Zambon defines his woman as an intercultural traveler. The mix, the cross-current mash-up of elements sampled from different, often opposing milieus—pop and high culture, street and elite, underground and mainstream, music and art—is the defining trait of his language. The rich range of inspirations is grafted, however, onto a formal base of classical rigor that owes a great deal to early Italian ready-to-wear in the dynamism of the lines, the functionalism of the solutions and the search for a timeless chic. This affinity, enriched by a touch of dry humor, is made even clearer if we consider that the designer indicates Yves Saint-Laurent, Coco Chanel, Franco Moschino and Rudi Gernreich as his own models of style, to whom he pays tribute with citations that are sometimes obvious, at others cryptic. "Each of my collections," explains Zambon, "stems from an organically spontaneous vision that brings together a series of inputs. In general I have two or three themes that I visualize already watered down on the woman as a final vision. From there I set off on my aesthetic and technical research into style and product. For example: Tropicália/Brazilian + Gordon Matta-Clark + 70s gay craziness and/or early hard rock. The result I aspire to is the definition of a sophisticated woman, timeless but abreast of the times, who knows how to choose her own style, not forgetting to exploit with intelligence her own femininity." Sergio Zambon attributes his love of the hybrid and the mixture to having grown up practically on a constant journey, bombarded by images and styles of different worlds. "I'm inspired by everything that is true, that has a strong aesthetic significance with a touch of distortion. I hate and at the same time aspire to balanced perfection. I mix atelier and industry, creativity and commerce, spontaneously keeping an eye on what is happening on the street and looking from the bottom up at what we want for ourselves, treated with the heritage of tailoring blended with industry." Zambon uses cryptic statements to define clothing that is clear. Paradoxically, the product, with its laconicism, often conceals the cultural richness of the process, reducing it to a vague but persistent vibration, a disturbing but barely perceptible note. It is the same sensation that you can get from looking at a picture by Hopper: everything is in its place, but the perfection generates disquiet, not serenity. Sergio Zambon distorts the classical with the same verve.(af)

Born in Egypt in 1965, he studied at the Istituto Europeo di Design in Rome. After graduating he joined the Fendi design office, where he worked on women's ready-to-wear and the Fendissime line. In parallel, he set himself up as a freelance consultant. With the entrance of Fendi into the LVMH group, he was designer of the Fendi Uomo line for six seasons, from 2006 al 2009. In 1997 he launched the Zambon line, put on ice in 2003 to allow him to devote himself to the project SoftCore. In 2009 he relaunched the collection in his name, now labeled Sergio Zambon, and presented it on the calendar at Milano Collezioni.

HALSTON, FW 2008-2009

HALSTON, FW 2008-2009

ROCHAS, FW 2009-2010

HALSTON, FW 2008-2009

HALSTON, FW 2008-2009

Marco Zanini

ROCHAS, FW 2009-2010

HALSTON, FW 2008-2009

HALSTON, FW 2008-2009

HALSTON, FW 2008-2009

HALSTON, FW 2008-2009

ROCHAS, FW 2009-2010

ROCHAS, FW 2009-2010

ROCHAS, SS 2010

ROCHAS, SS 2010

ROCHAS, FW 2009-2010

ROCHAS, SS 2010

ROCHAS, SS 2010

Defining the work of a designer who has played crucial roles, but supporting ones, in authoritative fashion houses, where his personal contribution has always been subjugated to the perfecting of an already formulated style, poses some difficulty. Reticence and eclecticism, in addition, generally characterize the approach taken by Marco Zanini, even when, as recently, his position has become more visible and his responsibility over the creative output total. The designer, however, does not submit passively to these two concepts; on the contrary, he acts on them with lucid awareness. His language is a delicate and subtle, impalpable one, the reflection of a reserved personality and the desire to communicate with the public in a way that is not obvious or ostentatious. "I cannot define my style," he declared. "I believe in the strong individuality of each person. I strive to offer a choice to those who do not wish to conform. Designing a collection is complex, multifaceted and exhilarating work. It arises from many different elements that come together to form the whole. Starting with the choice of fabrics and colors, then thinking about how to apply them and in what forms, and ending by defining their styling. The idea that lies at the root of the process and guides the craft is an inspiration. It is usually a path that one chooses to take without an apparent compass except the abstract feeling that it's the right one." Zanini likes clean lines, the work of paring down, but he is not a minimalist. He contradicts the purity of the design and the clarity of the silhouette with the choice of languid materials–brocade, lamé, jacquard silk–with a sometimes solid, sometimes liquid feel that create unexpected balances and imbalances, accentuated by surprising details and touches of romantic, controlled casualness. The choice of odd, sophisticated colors, arranged in startling compositions, is highly original, but the touch is always light and spontaneous, not strained. "Everything that is classic is modern. What in particular is modern today, however, I really don't know. I believe that the exclusive preoccupation with proposing modernity often produces barren results," he concludes. "Fashion is a complex language and a craft; it is not art and it is not just commerce. Balancing fantasy and reality is our precise task as designers." (af)

Marco Zanini

Born in Milan in 1971, he studied at the Accademia di Belle Arti di Brera. He collaborated with Lawrence Steele and then joined the team at Dolce & Gabbana as an assistant to Domenico Dolce for the women's wear collection. Moving to the Versace fashion house, he stayed there for nine years, working alongside Donatella Versace as head designer of women's *prêt-à-porter* and *haute couture*. At the end of 2007 he moved to New York, where he became creative director for the relaunch of Halston. In July 2008 he was appointed creative director of the Rochas house. He presented his first collection in Paris in March 2009. In October of the same year the line made its debut on the catwalks in Paris.

Photolitography
Fotolito Veneta, San Martino Buonalbergo (VR)

Printed by
Grafiche SIZ s.p.a., Campagnola di Zevio (VR)
for Marsilio Editori® s.p.a., Venice

edition

10   9   8   7   6   5   4   3   2   1

year

2011   2012   2013   2014   2015